EDWARD E. LOWINSKY

12 January 1908–11 October 1985

In the Fall of 1983, the College of Fine Arts and Communications at Brigham Young University invited Professor Edward Lowinsky, Ferdinand Schevill Distinguished Service Professor Emeritus at the University of Chicago, to inaugurate the new series of Dean's Lectures. He graciously assented and favored us with a lecture of broad scope and conception, a lecture that harmonized perfectly with our College's encompassing interests in the arts.

At the conclusion of Professor Lowinsky's visit, I proposed that the College publish his lecture in an expanded form as a fine print book to be given as a gift to his colleagues in the American Musicological Society, to deans of colleges of fine arts throughout the country, and to other interested scholars. In this way, we would insure that his work would be known to a wide audience, and we would also commemorate this special occasion. Professor Lowinsky agreed to the proposal and set about the task of expanding, recasting, and further perfecting his lecture—a task that occupied him throughout 1984 and the first part of 1985.

It is lamentable that Professor Lowinsky's untimely death prevented him from seeing his monograph in its printed form, but he was able to complete the text and approve it for publication. Throughout the final stages of production, the monograph has enjoyed the scrupulous care of Professor Lowinsky's wife, Dr. Bonnie J. Blackburn, and I wish to express my deepest appreciation for her invaluable assistance and patience.

Cipriano de Rore's Venus Motet: Its Poetic and Pictorial Sources must now serve not only the cause of scholarship but also as a lasting celebration of a scholar passionately committed to this cause. As he words it in his credo:

Nothing great has ever been accomplished without passion and patience. Rooted in the same Latin word, *pati* (to suffer, to endure), passion and patience touch the two poles of the key element in a life that matters: commitment.

Please accept this little book with the compliments of the College.

Sincerely yours,

James A Mason

James A. Mason
Dean

Cipriano de Rore's Venus Motet

Cipriano de Rore's Venus Motet

ITS POETIC AND PICTORIAL SOURCES ❦ EDWARD E. LOWINSKY

To Bonnie

Contents

Preface

This paper was read in a condensed and an expanded form at Brigham Young University as "The Inaugural Dean's Lecture" in the College of Fine Arts and Communications: condensed as far as the text is concerned, expanded inasmuch as the Chamber Singers under the direction of Dr. Ronald Staheli performed Cipriano's motet both at the beginning and at the end of the lecture. I was asked to choose an interdisciplinary topic. This request had as much to do with the choice of the subject as my own inclination. The present paper will confine itself to the text of Rore's motet, since it is the text that led to the discovery of the poetic and pictorial sources of the work. The motet is available in Bernhard Meier's edition of the *Opera omnia* of Cipriano de Rore. A shortened version of the paper was presented at the Annual Meeting of the American Musicological Society in Philadelphia, October 1984, in a session chaired by Professor James Haar of the University of North Carolina at Chapel Hill.

I am deeply indebted to James A. Mason, Dean of the College, and Professor Thomas J. Mathiesen, Head of the Musicology Area in the Department of Music at Brigham Young University, for the honor of having been invited to give the inaugural lecture for the new series of Dean's Lectures at Brigham Young, for the warmth of their reception, the generosity of their hospitality, and last but not least for the privilege of having this paper published under the imprint of their University in a form that exceeds the author's fondest hopes. That they should have decided to send the paper out as a gift to the members of the American Musicological Society is more than its modest contents deserve. The publication would not have been possible in its present form without the help of Professor Martin Raish of the Department of Art at Brigham Young University. Professor Raish gave unstintingly of his time and energy to obtain photocopies in black and white and ektachrome transparencies of the paintings discussed in this paper, reproductions of unsurpassed excellence. It was a triumph of patience and diplomacy to persuade the authorities of the Dresden Museum of Art to let us have a color reproduction of Girolamo Carpi's *Venus*, something that I had not been able to achieve in thirty years.

My colleague, Howard M. Brown, Ferdinand Schevill Distinguished Service Professor of the

University of Chicago, aided me substantially by loaning me two microfilms of concordant sources. I benefitted also from his sympathetic and attentive reading of the paper. Professor Arthur W. H. Adkins, Edward Olson Professor in the Department of Classical Languages and Literatures at the University of Chicago, had the kindness to submit my translations of poems from the Latin to his keen critical eye. The footnotes will record some of his sage and erudite commentaries. Professor Mathiesen's sharp editorial eye caught a number of inconsistencies. To all three gentlemen I wish to express my warmest thanks.

If this paper does not carry on the title page the name of Bonnie J. Blackburn as my collaborator, it is only because of her friendly, but insistent refusal. It owes more than I can say to her infinite patience, her constant scrutiny of every thought and every word, and her vigilant and intelligent criticism. She rescued me from many a mistake and oversight. I dedicate the paper to her.

Rore's Venus Motet

Venus, in the words of Edith Hamilton, in her incomparable book on *Mythology*, was "the Goddess of Love and Beauty, who beguiled all, gods and men alike; the laughter-loving goddess, who laughed sweetly or mockingly at those her wiles had conquered; the irresistible goddess who stole away even the wits of the wise."[1] Even this brief description suffices to reveal the uniqueness of the neo-Latin poem set to music of five parts by Cipriano de Rore in the mid-sixteenth century in which we find the laughter-loving goddess weeping.[2] Here is the text accompanied by the translation I was able to wrest from the subtle language of the poem and a simple Latin prose version:

> Hesperiae cum laeta suas inviserat urbes,
> Venit ad Eridani ditia regna Venus,
> Et modo divitias miratur fertilis agri,
> Et modo Atestini moenia clara ducis.
> Hic amnis pulchram vidit sub imagine formam,
> Et pictum in tabula noscere credit opus.
>
> Quis mihi te similem pinxit, mea dulcis imago?
> Sola meos vultus quam bene ficta refers.
> Vera mea effigies, ait, est: hic vultus, et ipsum
> Pectus, et os, eadem lumina, labra, manus.
> Hanc postquam Eridani nympham cognovit, obortis
> Sic fata est lachrymis, quid iuvat esse deam?[3]

In simple Latin prose:

> Cum Venus laeta inviserat suas urbes,
> Venit ad ditia regna Eridani,
> Et modo miratur divitias fertilis agri,
> Et modo moenia clara ducis Atestini.

Hic vidit pulchram formam sub imagine amnis.
Et credit noscere opus pictum in tabula.

Quis pinxit te similem mihi, mea dulcis imago?
Quam bene, sola ficta, refers meos vultus.
Vera est effigies mea, ait: hic vultus, et pectus
Ipsum, et os, eadem lumina, labra, manus.
Postquam cognovit hanc nympham Eridani, sic fata est
Obortis lachrymis, quid iuvat esse deam?

In translation:

As Venus was happily visiting Italy's cities,
She came to the wealthy regions of the Po.
And now she marvels at the richness of the fertile land,
And now at the shining city of the Duke of Este.
Here she saw a beautiful figure on the painting of a river
And she believes she recognizes the work painted on the panel.

"Who painted you, my sweet image, so much like me?
How well you represent my features, being but handmade [*sola ficta*]!
It is," she said, "my true likeness:
Here are the face, the very breasts and mouth,
And here my eyes, my lips and hands."
Having thereupon recognized her as the nymph of the river Po,
She breaks out in tears:
"What use is it to be a goddess?"

Two passages posed particular difficulties in translation. The first two words of line 5 of the first stanza, "Hic amnis," seem clearly to mean "this river." But what sense would the line then make? 7

"This river saw a beautiful figure under the image . . ."; under what image? The poem does not say. Latin differs from many tongues in its freedom of word order. If we recast the line in simple prose, *hic* and *amnis* are separated: "Hic vidit pulchram formam sub imagine amnis." In the prose version "hic" would mean "here," and the subject of "vidit" would be "she," that is, Venus. Hence we obtain the following sentence: "Here she saw a beautiful figure on the painting of a river." This makes sense.

More difficult is the second passage, the fifth line of the second stanza. Now the problem is not grammar, but meaning: "Having thereupon recognized her as the nymph of the river Po." Who is the nymph of the river Po? What is she doing here? The poem offers no answers to these questions.

But there can be no mystery to the last line of the poem, ending in the desperate cry: "quid iuvat esse deam?" "What use is it to be a goddess?"—the meaning being: "What use is it to be a goddess, if mere mortals can recreate my beauty, trait for trait?" And Venus weeps. These are tears of jealousy such as Venus was wont to elicit from the eyes of mortals, not to shed herself. How can we explain them? The answer to this question forms part of the present paper.

The musical setting, for five voices, is the work of Cipriano de Rore, composer at the court of Ferrara from about 1545 to 1559, when Duke Ercole II died. He was famous above all as a madrigal composer who, following in the footsteps of his master Willaert, gave the decisive impulse to expressive rendering of the words.[4] Rore was also one of the finest motet composers of the century. His Venus motet was published in Venice by the illustrious music printer Antonio Gardane in the third book of the master's motets, in 1549.

Venus on the River Po: Cossa and Carpi

Rore's motet is a unique musical compliment to the Venus paintings with which Italian art of the Renaissance abounded. But was it a general compliment, or did the poet have a specific painting in mind? The text mentions particular places, the river Po and the city of the Duke of Este. That city is of course Ferrara; it lies near the Po, and it is called "shining" perhaps in reference to the Palazzo degli Diamanti built by Ercole I (reigning from 1471 to 1505). The palace took its name from the 12,600 slabs of marble cut into facets like diamonds, out of which it is constructed.[5] Ercole's favorite device was the diamond.

The court of Ferrara had a number of fine painters, the brothers Battista and Dosso Dossi, Benvenuto Garofalo, and Girolamo Carpi among them.[6] The dukes also commissioned works by such outstanding artists as Bellini, Raphael, Michelangelo, and Titian.[7] The text of Rore's motet offers an additional hint by placing Venus in a river scene. Can such a painting be found in Ferrara? One like it adorns the Palazzo Schifanoia. This magnificent structure was begun at the end of the fourteenth century; the name has the same significance (*schiva noia*) as the Potsdam palace "Sans souci" (carefree) that Frederick the Great had built for his leisure hours.[8] It took generations to complete the Palazzo Schifanoia and to adorn it with frescoes, the most famous of which is the cycle depicting the twelve months of the year, whose rich astrological symbolism has been disclosed in arresting detail by Aby Warburg, the father of modern iconography:

> Each month is shown in three parallel pictorial planes, one above the other, each with its own pictorial space and figures of half lifesize. The gods of Olympus in triumphal cars move on the highest plane; on the lowest the earthly goings-on at the court of Duke Borso are narrated; the middle space belongs to the world of astral divinities.[9]

Among the twelve months, the one by Francesco Cossa[10] illustrating April shows Venus on the river Po sitting on a throne placed on a mighty shell drawn by two swans. Before her kneels, vanquished and in chains, Mars, the God of War (see Pl. 1 for the fresco and Pl. 2 for a detail of Venus and Mars). Warburg shows how Cossa's Aphrodite is based, paradoxical as it may seem, on a tract dealing with the pagan gods written by Albericus, an English monk in the twelfth century, the *De deorum imaginibus libellus*, known also under the modern name Mythographus III. Cossa's Venus wears a wreath of white and red roses, doves flutter about her, she is riding on water, the three Graces accompany her, and Cupid is represented on her girdle as shooting at two lovers. All of these figures and symbols appear in Albericus's description.[11]

But Cossa's fresco cannot be the painting of which Rore's motet speaks. Venus is fully dressed; the text of Rore's work describes her as at least partially naked. The poem does not allude to Mars. Nor does the time frame fit. Cossa died circa 1478, almost three generations earlier than Cipriano de Rore.

Fortunately, there is another Venus painting that meets all our requirements. Its creator, Girolamo Carpi, is a contemporary of Rore, a fellow artist at the court of Ferrara; his Venus conceals none of her beauty, and the painting indeed shows a river scene (see Pl. 3). The goddess, as befits her rank, is accompanied by a group of three nymphs. An Italian art historian has recognized in the background the hills and trees of the landscape of Ferrara,[12] and thus we know that the river must be the Po.

Why does Venus stand on a shell-like boat driven by a wheel? "Stand" seems hardly the right word: her body is swaying to the right, her left arm stretched out as if to regain her balance. The wind appears to have driven her to the bank of the river and have blown her gown off sufficiently to reveal her figure almost completely. The little winged Cupid, "Eros" according to Greek mythology, a son of Venus, also seems to strive for equilibrium; while Venus rests her weight on her left foot, the little fellow stands on his right, and while she moves her right foot, he does the same with his left in a perfect counterpoint to his mother's movements. A similar *contrapposto* is shown in the two swans, one dashing forward, the other looking backward. The three nymphs are seated, two facing the viewer, one almost frontally, the other in three-quarter profile, the third in the middle offering her back to the beholder. She shares Venus's wind-driven motion and appears to hold on to her companion as if to steady herself.

11

The painting, now in the Staatliche Gemäldegalerie in Dresden, belongs to a group of works that the Elector of Saxony purchased from the duke of Modena in 1746. In an inventory of 1743 it is described in the following words: "a painting with a Galatea in a shell drawn by two swans with the train of Nymphs and Nereids" ("un quadro con una Galatea in una conchiglia tirata da due Cigni, col corteggio di Ninfe e Nereidi").[13] Felton Gibbons has proposed that the painting is a product of the collaboration between Battista Dossi (Venus) and Carpi ("the three swimming nudes"), and he ascribes the Cupid and the swans, for stylistic reasons, to "the seventeenth or eighteenth centuries." He regards the description in the inventory of 1743, which omits mention of the Cupid, as suggesting "that the painting of the Cupid may postdate 1743 and that the later alterations were designed to change the iconography."[14]

A number of questions arise from this conclusion:

1. Must we look at the characterization of an inventory as if it were the careful description of an art critic? It could happen even to Vasari in speaking of Botticelli "that the two compositions had merged in his mind to such an extent that he transferred the Cupid from the 'Primavera' to the *Birth of Venus* (while at the same time pluralizing him) and, on the other hand, transferred the action of adorning the goddess with flowers from the Zephyrs in the *Birth of Venus* to the self-contented Graces in the 'Primavera'."[15] If the greatest historian and connoisseur of the art of the Cinquecento can commit such errors, is it reasonable to assume that a mere listing of a painting by an anonymous official can be treated as if it constituted a serious description of a work of art by an expert? More important, is it correct that the identification of the subject in the inventory as "Galatea" rules out the figure as Venus? Again, we must be careful not to treat an accountant as if he were a connoisseur. Whoever did not know the true history of Carpi's Venus, about which below, saw it quite naturally as the painting of a nymph, a Galatea, and under this name it might well have been known among the servants at court.[16]

2. Whereas the iconographic significance of the swans in connection with Venus is well established for the fifteenth and sixteenth centuries, it would be interesting to see whether

seventeenth- and eighteenth-century paintings and iconologies are still familiar with it.[17]

3. Does the precise rhythmic counterpoint that we see between the movements of Venus and her son not rather argue for a careful design of the original inventor?

4. And above all: how could the painter have presented Venus pulling an arrow from Cupid's quiver with her right hand if there was no Cupid? This question is not touched upon by Gibbons. Nor does Gibbons deal with the spatial consequences in removing Cupid. *With* Cupid we have a sequence of five persons, so closely grouped that they are in actual or virtual physical contact with each other: actual contact between the first two nymphs over water and the second and third ones under water; the third nymph's elbow seems to touch Cupid's left foot at the heel, while his right foot virtually touches Venus's right foot and his hand his mother's arm: the chain of human contact and motion is carefully calculated. *Without* Cupid, the chain is broken and a vacuum emerges with no evident justification. It is as if a stream of magnetism flowing through this group were suddenly interrupted.[18]

As to the dual ascription, Felton Gibbons was unaware of the literary evidence presented below in the Excursus, which unequivocally connects the painting with Carpi alone.

Further Antecedents of Carpi's Venus Painting

Most of the details of the painting can be explained if we return to Edith Hamilton's description of Venus (or, as the Greeks call her, Aphrodite):

. . . [Aphrodite] is said to have sprung from the foam of the sea. . . . *Aphros* is foam in Greek. This sea-birth took place near Cythera, from where she was wafted to Cyprus. Both islands were ever after sacred to her, and she was called Cytherea or the Cyprian as often as by her proper name. One of the Homeric Hymns, calling her "Beautiful, golden goddess," says of her:

> The breath of the west wind bore her
> Over the sounding sea,
> Up from the delicate foam,
> To wave-ringed Cyprus, her isle.[19]

We now see why Venus appears on a shell in the water, why Carpi depicts her swaying in the wind, and why sea nymphs accompany her on the journey to Italy. Swans are associated with Venus in the fresco of Francesco Cossa. That they go back to ancient Greek mythology is shown by a painting on an Attic wine jug from the end of the fifth century B.C. (see Pl. 4).[20] In the center is Venus, attended by two Erotes—the Greek counterparts of the Roman Cupids—and surrounded in strictly symmetrical order by two women, Nereids, riding on dolphins, two male figures, to the left Dionysus with the thyrsos staff, to the right Hermes with the herald's staff, and at the end two seated sea nymphs. Nereids are daughters of the "old sea god" Nereus. Venus and the swan are shown at the moment when the goddess emerges from the waves; it is, as the Greek name calls her, "Aphrodite Anadyomene." The waves are suggested in the small white half-circles at the bottom of the painting, which is generally attributed to the workshop of the potter Meidias, flourishing in the last part of the fifth and the beginning of the fourth century B.C.[21] If it be asked whether we can presume so far-reaching an interest on Carpi's part in ancient painting and motives, his Roman sketchbook gives a conclusive answer. Made available only recently, it is a comprehensive and diversified collection of drawings of antique models, partly from originals, partly from copies of antiques by Raphael and other masters of his circle.[22]

Finally, we have proof that the idea of showing Venus on a shell goes back to Greek art as well. The Louvre owns a *terra cotta* figurine of a nude Aphrodite kneeling on a shell from the fifth century B.C. (Pl. 5). To suggest how frequent this motive was in Greek sculpture, the first student of this statuette, Paul Jamot, began his essay with these words: "Tous les musées possèdent des statuettes de terre cuite représentant Vénus sous les traits d'une femme nue agenouillée entre les valves d'une coquille marine."[23]

Any work of art, to be fully understood, must be placed into its context, both backward and forward. The most famous predecessor of Carpi's Venus painting is Botticelli's *Birth of Venus*, variously dated as between 1478 and 1487, but at any rate about two generations earlier than Carpi's (see Pl. 6).[24] In the middle stands Venus on a shell, having been brought to the shore by two winged wind gods, Zefiro and Clori, whose currents of air blown from full cheeks cause the goddess's golden hair to flutter. To the right, one of the *Horae*, the four Seasons, stands ready to clothe her in a magnificent scarlet-colored mantle embroidered with black stars. Fortunately for posterity, she is just one moment too late. Botticelli's topic is the same as Carpi's: Venus's birth from the sea.

The contrast between Cossa's dressed and Botticelli's and Carpi's nude Venus has a background, which Panofsky discusses in his studies of Titian's paintings of Venus. In medieval art, he explains, "the juxtaposition of two women, similar in appearance," of whom "one is nude, the other draped," means that "the draped figure stands for a saintly or lofty principle whereas the nude evoked, if not the idea of carnal pleasure, at least the idea of the natural . . . state of man. . . . In the Renaissance, however, nudity became an attribute of positive principles—not only of Truth but also, to give a selection from Ripa [*Iconologia*, 1593], of such exalted concepts as Feminine Beauty, Genius (*Ingegno*), Friendship, Soul, Clarity or Radiance (*Chiarezza*), and Eternal as opposed to Transient Bliss." Ripa distinguishes between "*Felicità Eterna* represented as 'a nude figure lifting a flame

17

heavenward'" and "*Felicità Breve* as 'a figure draped in white and yellow, adorned with precious stones. . . .'"[25] Panofsky's interpretation finds a magnificent confirmation in Botticelli's *Calumny of Apelles.*[26] "Truth" is personified by the nude figure of a young woman looking heavenward and lifting one arm upward in a gesture of imploring divine aid, "Calumny" by the ugly figure of an old hag, draped in black, turning backward and fixing "Truth" with a hateful gaze. Ronald Lightbown places the painting in a chapter subtitled "Botticelli and Savonarola."

One may view the Botticelli painting as representative of the High Renaissance and Carpi's of the succeeding period of mannerism. In accordance with the stress on motion, Carpi's manneristic conception gives us a figure of Venus in full swing, as it were. Botticelli's Venus, on the other hand, is shown in calm balance, leaving the element of motion symmetrically to the left with the winds, and to the right with the gown of the Season and Aphrodite's mantle that she carries. Carpi's scene is crowded, Botticelli's has plenty of free space—it leaves air to breathe in. To put it into a simplified formula: the ideas of balance, symmetry, harmony are characteristic for the High Renaissance; those of stress, motion, dissonance belong to the period of mannerism.[27] That Carpi's painting treads lightly on dissonance shows F. Antal's acuteness of judgment in placing him between classicism and mannerism.

The difference of character shows also in light and color. Ronald Lightbown says of this painting: "There is no more radiant picture in European art than this,"[28] and he has in mind the intense light and the play of white, gold, and red; Carpi's painting uses darker tonalities, a reddish brown, a greenish yellow, a subdued blue in the background, and a chromatic accompaniment, the yellowish light of the cloud streaking from one side of the picture to the other—a light that seems reflected in one of the swans, one of the nymphs, and the illuminated side of Venus's body. These paintings, separated by two generations, illustrate on the one hand thematic unity inspired by identical antique sources, on the other entirely different interpretations of the antique myth and different conceptions of space, color, and motion.

18   Botticelli has created a figure of paradoxical propensities, alluring and innocent, tempting and

chaste, revealing and concealing. None of the Venus paintings, past or future, have that particular ambiguity, Titian's magnificent figures least of all. If there is a model for Botticelli's goddess, it comes from ancient Greece; it is the *Venus Pudica.* Margarete Bieber, in her book on Greek and Roman art, writes: "Aphrodite appears in Hellenistic and Roman art with her drapery knotted before her lap. . . . The Roman copyists liked to show Venus with the motif introduced by the school of Praxiteles in the Aphrodite Medici. Here, the goddess covers her breast with one hand, and with her other her lap, in a gesture of modesty."[29] Bieber's Fig. 233 seems to be the type Botticelli had in mind. The statue in Fig. 233 is defective; the right arm is broken off above the elbow; but the three points of support that would normally not be seen (1, on the left side in the middle below the breasts, 2, on the upper part of the left arm, 3, high on the left side of the left arm) indicate that the right arm was covering the left breast. Fortunately, a beautiful Greek original is preserved intact in the Uffizi in Florence (see Pl. 7).[30] Botticelli must have been familiar with one of the many figures of *Venus Pudica.* But he replaced the mantle of the Roman or the hand of the Greek sculptors with the wave of rich golden hair flowing down from her head. This, too, had an ancient tradition, albeit in a significant variation. In his illuminating study on "The *Anadyomene* in the Mediaeval Tradition," W. S. Heckscher shows an astonishing "Gold and Lapis Lazuli Pendant" of the early seventh century, probably of Egyptian provenance (Fig. 2), representing Aphrodite Anadyomene standing in a shell and holding up two rich strands of hair with both hands, while a fold of tunic covers one leg and her pudenda.[31] Botticelli painted three Venus figures, all in tempera.[32] Two of these have the motif of the hair replacing mantle or hand. However, Botticelli borrowed no more than a gesture from the *Venus Pudica,* important as that is. Nothing in the Greek model gives the slightest presentiment of the richness, the depth, the paradoxical tensions in Botticelli's Venus. A great work of art is always a confluence of a multiplicity of influences. According to Aby Warburg, Botticelli was inspired by the poem of Botticelli's contemporary and co-citizen, Angelo Poliziano, whose *La Giostra* contains descriptions of Venus's birth astonishingly similar to Botticelli's painting.[33] E. H. Gombrich, on the other hand, developed the theory that the painting was done according to a lost humanistic program, the center of which was Ficino's idea that Venus was the embodiment of *Humanitas*. [34] Lightbown gives a history of literary sources. [35]

Titian's Venus Paintings: Love and Music

The peak of Italian Venus paintings was reached by Titian. "Girolamo [Carpi] knew Titian well personally, and undoubtedly the works he made for Ferrara; by order of Ercole II he had even copied, for the King of France, his very grandseigneurial *Portrait of Alfonso I*."[36] Also, a musicological study must not overlook the one painter who associates Venus almost consistently with music. In Titian's Venus figures, Love and Music seem inseparable.[37]

It is the consensus of Titian scholars that "Venus with a lutenist" (Pl. 8) is the last of the four paintings of Venus with a musician, about ten to fifteen years later than the Venus paintings with an organist. In a famous article, Otto Brendel has taken the view that "there is no apparent sign of mutual understanding between the two main characters. The lady simply pays no attention, and it is doubtful that she even hears the music which, one feels, is not played for her ears."[38] In order to arrive at this conclusion—I am not aware that it was ever challenged in the huge literature on this painting[39]—Brendel had to overlook, temporarily, the flute (recorder) Venus is holding in her hand and the viola da gamba that leans against the pillows on which she is resting.[40] But if the lutenist is serenading a beautiful lady who is holding a flute in her hands, does it not mean that a while earlier they had played a duet together? And does the viola da gamba not suggest that the two might also have played (or will soon play) a duet of lute and a low-tuned string instrument together?[41]

An art historian may be forgiven for demanding visual contact, if he is to concede "mutual understanding" between two players. A musician, on the other hand, knows that contact between musicians is established more by the ear than by the eye. A music historian, familiar with painted music scenes, is further aware that the listeners shown are not necessarily looking at the musician. In Raphael's "Parnassus," for example, we find Apollo playing the lira da braccio on Mount Parnassus, where the Castelian spring flows; he is surrounded by a crowd of laurel-crowned figures, Homer and Dante leading both ancient and modern poets; Apollo is attended by the nine Muses. All of them are divided into diverse groups, most of them listening, a few conversing. But among the dozens of devotees we count no more than three Muses gazing intently at Apollo, who looks

22

heavenward, playing in the grip of inspiration.

More than three hundred years later, a modern Apollo, Franz Liszt, appears in the famous painting by Joseph Danhauser (1840).[42] The scene takes place in an elegant Parisian salon. Liszt sits at the piano, improvising (the music sheets on the piano notwithstanding), looking upward, like Raphael's Apollo, in the company of Alexandre Dumas, Victor Hugo, George Sand, Paganini, Rossini, and the Countess Marie d'Agoult. Not a single one of the listeners looks at the pianist. Even Paganini and Rossini, who stand close to the piano, do not look at Liszt; they are absorbed in listening, their eyes fixed into the room's wide space. George Sand is sitting on a leather chair casting her eyes upward with an ecstatic expression on her face, the Countess is sitting at the feet of her beloved Franz, looking down—one sees only her back—probably eyes closed. Dumas and Hugo, the former sitting, the latter standing, are looking pensively into the void, images of devoted listening. The modern concert hall, in which the musicians play on an elevated stage, the auditorium dark, bright lights concentrating on the stage, has changed all that. The audience has now no choice but to look at the musicians on stage. Whether this has contributed to increasing the listeners' concentration on the music is another question.

Brendel seeks in vain for predecessors of the four paintings of Venus with musicians and concludes: "This is not a common theme of Renaissance painting."[43] While it is indeed not a common theme of Renaissance painting, it is not entirely without precedent. Brendel confined himself to Venice. But Titian paid several visits to Ferrara. There he might have picked up, if not the theme, at least motives for his later Venus paintings. Alfonso must have shown his guest Francesco Cossa's fresco of "Venus and Mars" in the Palazzo Schifanoia (see Plate 1). Surely, the young and impressionable artist, a music enthusiast throughout his life, studied the work with care and made mental notes, perhaps even sketches, involving Venus and the crowd of Venus worshippers with recorders, lutes, and a rebec (a bowed string instrument of medieval origin) in their hands. These instruments are assigned to young women, all paired with young men. On the left side the lady holding the rebec is being embraced and kissed by her lover. On the right, the two young beauties, one holding a pair of recorders, the other a lute, are in the company of a young nobleman, standing behind them, resting his hands on their shoulders. On the same side to the forefront, another musician holds a lute and she appears to join with a young man standing so close that their bodies, arms, and legs seem to touch. They gaze at a couple kneeling on the ground, the lady allowing her lover the freest expression of amorous touch. All these are symbols of the union of Venus and music.[44] An original stroke is Titian's transposition of the music scene from the large to the small, from the noble to the vulgar: far removed in the middle ground nude forest creatures dance to the tune of the bagpipe played by a satyr leaning against a tree.

Harold E. Wethey, who consulted the eminent musicologist Emanuel Winternitz, gave a very different interpretation of the picture. He says of Venus that "she holds a recorder as she appears to pause while Cupid places a wreath upon her head."[45] Winternitz included in his analysis the "Fitzwilliam Venus" in Cambridge (a copy attributed by Wethey to "Titian and Workshop"[46]) because it offers further musical details: two part-books, one closed, directed toward the viewer and labelled TENOR, the other turned toward Venus and containing a bassus part (which is supposed to be used by Venus when she plays the viola da gamba). David Rosand accords music a dominating place in the New York painting; above all, he has Venus participate in music-making:

> Having established the type of Venus with an organist—which would be repeated in several studio versions—Titian later wrought one final variation on the theme, changing the musician to a lute player (colorplate 40). And with the introduction of that socially and physically more adaptable instrument he expanded the musical significance of the image, for now Venus herself, with a recorder, participates in an ensemble; crowned the goddess of beauty, she is nonetheless accessible not only to the senses but through the social experience of music-making as well.[47]

Winternitz, following Brendel, believes that the flute is not an attribute of Venus—and this is certainly true. Yet, there are ancient sources that allude to some associations between Venus and the flute. One we owe to Wethey, who quotes a poem from the *Greek Anthology*[48] in which Opis,

24

"having been vanquished by love for beautiful Bryson," offered a silver flute to Aphrodite wrought by himself.[49] Would Opis have offered his flute to Aphrodite, had he not good reason to believe that the goddess would appreciate his gift?

Another ancient source confirming an association between Venus and the flute has been uncovered by Gombrich, who in his discussion of Botticelli's "Primavera," refers to Apuleius in "The Golden Ass," describing the competition between Juno, Pallas Athena, and Venus for Paris's judgment:

> And lo, now Venus, amidst the applause of the audience, smiling sweetly, stands right in the middle of the stage, surrounded by the gayest crowd of boys. . . . Already the melodious flutes sounded luxurious Lydian harmonies, melting the hearts of the audience with their sweetness—but far sweeter still, Venus began placidly to move with a hesitating, slow step, gently swaying her body, slightly inclining her head, and with delicate gestures responded to the voluptuous sound of the flutes. . . .[50]

Titian's Venus with a flute is perhaps not quite without ancient roots. Winternitz wonders what the viola da gamba is doing in Titian's painting and concludes: "no Venus is known to play a viola da gamba, or indeed any instrument."[51] This would seem to rule out Titian's painting as evidence. To justify his conclusion, Winternitz questions whether the beautiful woman is indeed Venus. He demotes Cupid to the role of a "winged *putto* in attendance," he overlooks his act of crowning his mother, and disregards the consensus of art historians that we have here as genuine a Venus as was ever painted. A genius of Titian's order of magnitude may allow himself a break with tradition here and there. Winternitz himself, a few pages earlier, wrote:

> art historians have often misunderstood or even disregarded the meaning and importance of the flute in some very famous paintings of the Italian Renaissance. While the flute is not part of the official, conventional, pictorial idiom or language of symbols as codified in the iconological,

25

mythographical, and emblematic treatises such as those by Ripa, Cartari, and Natalis Comes, it nonetheless appears so frequently as a conspicuous and unequivocal accessory in paintings with amorous topics that there can be no doubt about its connotation.[52]

When he comes to the fresco of Francesco Cossa and the *flauti dolci* (recorders) held by the girl in the center, "directly over the amorous couple," he says: "The iconophile, confronted by the attributes of Venus in the same fresco, will not regard the flauti dolci as accidental."[53] What more help do we need?

Without disclaiming his initial position, Brendel, through a process of rigorous comparison of Titian's Venus presentations preceding *Venus and the Lutenist* (named the "Holkham Venus"), arrives eventually at a very different view. Now he asks: "Why does she hold a flute?" And he finds that "the musical implements around her in these paintings [New York and Cambridge] stress the point more than did the other versions. . . . The reclining goddess, crowned by love, is here equipped to exhibit the common 'celestial' origin of both visual and aural beauty. . . . The representation of Venus comes near to a simple personification of music."[54]

Brendel includes the landscape in his iconographic description. He refers to Panofsky's idea of *paysages moralisées*. Departing from "the device, common in late-mediaeval and Renaissance painting, of dividing the landscape background into two halves of symbolically contrasting character," Panofsky proposes to call '*paysage moralisée*' that landscape in which the "'Aera sub lege' is contrasted with the 'Aera sub gratia'." Using this felicitous concept, Brendel sees "the allusions to music prevail in the landscape as well. The swans at the left, birds of Apollo, are easily associated with song. In the level land to the right of the lute players, people dance to the music under the trees. . . . Apollo dislikes the sound of the flute to which they dance. If, as might well be, the distinction is intentional, it can have moralizing implications. . . ."[55]

One is tempted to conclude that this may account for the extraordinary attention given to the

background and its enchanting iridescent play of colors. To a great artist the painterly problem is at least as interesting as its symbolic value.

In a new and important book, Lewis Lockwood sees Cossa's Venus and Mars fresco as a "commentary on the theme of the garden of love, in which music always had a role to play and was regarded as an erotic stimulus, as in contemporary literary references."[56] This means, I fear, to misunderstand the medieval theme of the garden of love and, *a fortiori*, that of Cossa's fresco, and no less the role of music. In the garden of love, as illustrated, for example, in the *Roman de la Rose*,[57] we find young people, singly or paired, stylishly dressed in a summer garden shaded by fruit-laden trees, a group of four making music, three singers (two ladies, one youth), one lutenist. They sing, presumably, of the beauty of nature, of youth and love. These handsome young people in the prime of life need no "erotic stimulus," they make music to express their *joie de vivre*. It is an idyllic scene without an element of strife. Cossa, to the contrary, presents the battle between the god of war and the goddess of love, the latter in full triumph, the former kneeling in chains and abject, if willing, defeat.

Lockwood continues: "it is as if the usual business of music-making, a relatively sober and temperate form of social recreation, temporarily stops during the moment that is depicted, to increase the shock of the erotic scene." Music in its finest manifestations is an ecstatic transformation of physical activity, singing and playing, into a higher form of human consciousness. Even in listening to a simple folk dance or a waltz by Johann Strauss, we feel transported by sound and rhythm, as do the dancers that are swept along on the dance floor. There is an element of spiritual intoxication in almost all music-making. *Nemo cantat sobrius*, says an early seventeenth-century writer,[58] and he certainly did not mean to say that only people under the influence of wine sing. Likewise, if the innocent lovers' play is an "erotic shock," then the literature of the Renaissance from Boccaccio to Shakespeare must be a continuous shock treatment rather than the delight it has been for generations of readers.

The association of Love and Music may well go back to St. Augustine, who called "Love music's master" (*Musicam docet amor*), a conceit favored by the Greek myth that the alliance between

27

Venus and Mars brought forth a daughter, "Harmonia."[59] This idea comes from Hesiod and was taken up by Boccaccio in his *Genealogia Deorum*.[60] The sentiment was spread throughout the world of the Renaissance by Erasmus, who accepted it in his immense collection of ancient proverbs, the *Adagia*, mentioned by Edgar Wind.[61] Augustine was probably influenced by Plato, who, in the *Symposium*, says: ". . . and thus music, too, is a science of the phenomena of love in their application to harmony and rhythm."[62] Augustine's book *De Musica* was printed many times in the fifteenth and sixteenth centuries, both in the *Opuscula plurima* and in *Omnium operum primus tomus*. But Augustine speaks about music in many of his other writings. There are few sentences more moving in the world's literature than his confession of the power that music exercises over his soul:

> Yet when it happens to me to be more moved by the singing than by what is sung, I confess myself to have sinned criminally. . . . See now the condition I am in! Weep with me, and weep for me. . . . But Thou, O Lord my God . . . have mercy upon me, and heal me—Thou, in whose sight I am become a puzzle to myself; and this is my infirmity.[63]

Cipriano de Rore's setting to music a poem in praise of a Venus painting by his Ferrarese fellow artist, Girolamo Carpi, according to Vasari a great music lover, led us to investigate the Italian painters' ties to music. We have found that the interrelationship between the two arts, as reflected in the Venus paintings at least of Cossa and Titian, is indeed strong. A few elements in the social life of the period promoting interplay between the two arts are the rise of secular music in the sixteenth century and its penetration into all layers of society, high and low; further, the flourishing of academies, in which artists of all spheres of work met and in which music demonstrated its superiority as the most social and socializing of the arts, the one that appealed to the widest circles of the populace; and finally, the affinity between Love and Music so strikingly expressed by the most musical of the Church Fathers, St. Augustine. Nor should we overlook a visual element: musical instruments, particularly those of the Renaissance, were themselves works of art and aroused the wonderment and delight of painters, who saw in them an inexhaustible fountain of variety in shapes of all sorts and sizes.

The Poetic Source of Rore's Venus Motet

We come now to the question of the poetic source of Rore's Venus motet, a question that has pursued me since I wrote my dissertation, in which I first referred to the work.[64] Keeping up my reading on Ferrarese art and literature, eventually I came across a collection of neo-Latin poems by Girolamo Falletti, humanist, ambassador, and confidant of the Duke of Ferrara.[65] There I found Rore's poem. The book was published in 1546; it carries the title *Hieronymi Phalethi Savonensis, Poematum libri septem.*[66] The collection contains a whole cycle of poems dealing with this painting, with Carpi, and with the model of Carpi's Venus, who is revealed as Anna d'Este, the daughter of the rulers of Ferrara, Ercole d'Este II and Renée (see Excursus). Anna's mother, a French-born princess, had the courage to keep her private court as an island of Protestantism in a Catholic duchy, a papal fief at that.[67]

Anna d'Este had enjoyed an extraordinarily fine education. Her and her sisters' musical instruction was in the hands of a French musician, Jean Milleville.[68] At the age of ten her Latin and Greek were good enough to enable her to make comparisons between Greek and Roman poets. The classical education that she and her two sisters, Lucrezia and Leonora, received prepared the young ladies, together with their brothers, to recite Terence's comedy *Adelphi* in the original Latin at the occasion of Pope Paul III's visit to Ferrara in 1544. Anna was then thirteen years old.[69] This is the time in which Carpi painted her as Venus on the river Po,[70] Falletti wrote his poems, and Rore composed his motet.[71]

Falletti's cycle of poems begins with an epigram that carries the title "In pictura[m] Annae principis Estensis" ("on a painting of Anna, Princess of Este").[72] The title discloses that the model of Carpi's Venus was Anna d'Este. Four other poems, including this one, are entitled: *Ad eandem* ("To the same"). We are offering the text of Rore's motet in the two editions of Girolamo Falletti of 1546 and 1557. The 1546 version is the main text; the revisions of 1557, tiny as they are, show the poet's meticulous hand (see notes). The parts of the text that deviate from that in Rore's motet are given in italics; changes in word order are not marked.

Hesperiae cum laeta suas *inviseret* urbes,
    Venit ad Eridani ditia regna Venus:
Et modo divitias miratur fertilis agri,
    Et modo Atestini moenia clara Ducis.[1]
Hinc[2] *tum forte tuam* vidit sub imagine formam[3]
    Et pictum in tabula noscere credit opus.

Quis mihi te similem pinxit, mea dulcis imago?
    Sola meos vultus quam bene *picta* refers!
Vera *mei* effigies, ait, est hic vultus, et ipsum
    Pectus, et os, eadem lumina, labra, manus.
Ut verò[4] Eridani Nympham *te agnovit,* obortis
    Sic fata est lacrimis,[5] quid iuvat esse Deam?

1) ducis 2) Hic 3) comma after formam 4) vero 5) lacrymis

Two passages of Falletti's poem differ substantially from Rore's text—precisely those that put obstacles in the way of translation and understanding. Where Rore's line 5 in stanza 1 has "Hic amnis pulchram vidit sub imagine formam" ("Here she saw a beautiful figure on the painting of a river"), Falletti gives "Hic[73] tum forte tuam vidit sub imagine formam" ("Here then by chance she saw your figure in a painting"), that is, Venus saw Anna's figure, her double, in a painting. The fifth line of Rore's second stanza reads "Hanc postquam Eridani nympham cognovit" ("Having thereupon recognized her as the nymph of the river Po"). Since we have not heard of the nymph of the river Po before, the passage is hard to understand. In Falletti's version the line reads "Ut vero Eridani Nympham te agnovit" ("But as she [Venus] recognized you [Anna] as the nymph of the river Po"). Already in the first stanza Anna, the subject and title of the poem, is addressed. Now she is referred to again and identified by Venus as nymph of the river Po—a quasi-divine patroness of the river. This means that in Falletti's version, Anna is not identified with Venus; she only looks like Venus. In Rore's motet, on the other hand, the figure on the shell is identified with Venus—a vital difference. The two passages that diverge from Falletti's poem are those that address Anna herself. In Falletti's wording they are perfectly clear; we have no reason to assume that they present the poet's earlier version. For reasons we do not know, Cipriano set a text that removed all references to Anna d'Este.[74] Interestingly enough, Falletti's version of these two passages does not fit Rore's music. Originally, the poem was a compliment to Anna; in its revised form, where Anna does not appear at all, it was a tribute to the unnamed painter. As such it has entered the musical literature.

Rore and the Court of Ferrara

Is it possible that Rore himself took the initiative to have Falletti's poem changed from a eulogy of Anna d'Este to praise of Girolamo Carpi? Let us consider the part of the evidence that might favor this theory. For one thing, we know that Carpi was a passionate music lover. In his essay on Carpi, Giorgio Vasari recalls conversations with the painter in Rome in the year 1550, during which Carpi confessed to have lost too much time in his youth in amorous adventures and in playing the lute, instead of having devoted himself seriously to painting.[75] And again, later, in summing up the personality of Carpi, Vasari stresses anew that "he took pleasure in music beyond measure."[76] Also, Carpi was responsible for the stage designs for some of Ferrara's famed theatrical representations, in which capacity he collaborated with Alfonso della Viola and Antonio del Cornetto.[77] It stands to reason that Carpi and Rore, having served at the same time at the same court, were on a personal and friendly footing. But is it thinkable that Rore would dare to change a text, bending it to favor the court painter rather than the noble model?

To this speaks a point largely overlooked by his biographers: Rore was something less than the perfect courtier. We have from him a letter containing a phrase that we would search for in vain in the correspondence of any other court musician of the Renaissance (or any other period) in a letter to his prince, and that, curiously enough, only one of his biographers, Alfred Einstein, has paid any attention to. This phrase is the more remarkable as it is part of a letter Rore wrote after the death of Ercole II to offer his continued services to the Duke's son, Alfonso II. The letter is dated as of the twelfth of November 1559 from Antwerp, home of his parents, whom he had already visited in 1558 and found in great misery. He says: "Now that I wanted to stay with my parents in freedom and quiet, I had found them, after my departure from there, ruined by diverse disasters that had befallen them, and I am forced to return to a new yoke."[78]

None of Rore's biographers, excepting Alfred Einstein, understood why Alfonso II ignored Rore's offer of service, yet even Einstein expressed his view in tentative terms.[79] But the astonishing passage in Rore's letter to Alfonso, in which the composer contrasted the freedom in his parents' house with the yoke he would have to bear in Alfonso's service, deserves to be taken seriously, not only for the composer's sake, but also for the sake of Alfonso II.[80] No prince of the Renaissance, offering an annual salary of 240 *scudi,* a rent-free home, and benefices[81] to his choirmaster, placing at his disposal an ensemble of accomplished musicians and an audience of the finest connoisseurs and music lovers, would tolerate having such a position characterized as a "yoke."[82] It took an extraordinary character and temperament to write the prince whose services he was seeking in such an unprecedented vein. Lodovico Ariosto (1474–1533), court poet of Ferrara, whose poems Rore frequently set to music, is known to have complained bitterly about the loss of personal liberty that goes together with service at the court. But his complaints are directed to his brother or to a friend, not to the duke.[83]

The portrait of Rore made by Hans Mielich, the court painter of Albrecht V of Bavaria, the patron of Orlando di Lasso, in the year 1558, when he was forty-two years old, shows a man of fiery temperament, of that Flemish spirit of independence that gave Charles V and Philip II such trouble in the uprising of the Netherlands and the agitated years preceding it (Pl. 9).[84] Alvin Johnson extends Hol's and Einstein's[85] observation that not a single one of his five madrigal books published in Venice carries a dedication, saying "[Rore] never wrote a dedication for any of his publications."[86] This is very rare and certainly confirms that Cipriano was not a man to court nobles or merchant princes.

The question might be raised whether all this would not have to yield to another kind of evidence: Rore dedicated a whole number of madrigals and a few motets to the families of the duchies he served, those of Ferrara and of Parma.[87] This might indeed be a considerable obstacle to our thesis, but only if we knew for certain that the pieces so dedicated were composed by Rore voluntarily and spontaneously rather than commissioned by his patrons. An interesting case is the chanson *En vos adieux* and its response, *Hellas, comment,* written, as Bernhard Meier convincingly demonstrates, at the time of Anna's departure for France to be married to François d'Aumale, son of the Duc de Guise.[88] Since Anna's leaving Ferrara was generally mourned, one might suppose that Cipriano wrote the farewell chanson spontaneously. But this is very unlikely. He would have normally asked an Italian poet to write a suitable text. But not only is the text written in French in accord with her mother's nationality and that of her future husband, the formal structure of the poem rules out any personal involvement of the composer. The text is not a "dialogue," as Meier believes,[89] for then the speakers would have to be Anna and her mother and sisters, who accompanied her as far as Mantua. The response, *Hellas, comment,* is indeed made by mother and sisters, but the first part is the address of a neutral party—something like the choir in a Greek tragedy—attempting to console those who remain behind. Surely Anna could not have said

> En vos adieux, dames, cessés voz pleurs
> Pour le retour d'une princess' en France.

Nor would these words be appropriate if Rore wanted to lament Anna's departure. Nevertheless, Rore gave the French text a very expressive setting, in which a chromatic passage occurs "in soprano and bass, to which Zarlino refers with approval, [and which] portrays tear-stained cheeks."[90]

Art historians have accumulated massive evidence proving that artists at Italian and other courts executed the orders of their princely patrons. More often than not their patrons gave them detailed programs worked out by humanists, which they had to follow to the letter. Why should it have been different for composers? The patrons would commission the court poets to write verses for certain occasions and then ask the court composers to set them to music. In other words, dedicatory pieces cannot be used as proof that Rore served his princes with heart and soul. They were part of his duties. When he was free to do what he wanted, in the publication of his madrigals, he showed his thirst for independence, as we saw, in the unusual abstention from dedicating his music to anyone.[91] In sum, there is enough evidence to allow the possibility that Rore might well have been the one to change Falletti's text from a praise of Anna's beauty to a eulogy on her painter's talent.

But there is another possibility. Perhaps the Duke and the Duchess of Ferrara did not favor a motet in which their daughter figured as Venus.[92] In this case Falletti may well have felt prompted to identify the subject of the painting as the nymph of the river Po. Carpi's Venus was then *not* identified with Anna d'Este but with a river nymph that only *looked* like Venus.[93] In this way Anna was transformed from Venus into a semi-divine protectress of the river Po, the native river of Ferrara—a not uncommon flattery in addressing members of a princely household. Falletti might have told the duke about a famous precedent set by antiquity, which was well known in the Renaissance through Pliny's *Natural History*. Alexander the Great had a "woman named Pankaspe, who was his principal favorite among all his concubines . . .; owing to his admiration for her beauty . . . [he had her] painted in the nude by Apelles. . . . There are those," says Pliny, "who believe that she was the model from whom the *Aphrodite Anadyomene* ["Rising from the Sea"] was painted."[94] But the duke undoubtedly felt what was fitting for Alexander's concubine was not necessarily fitting for his daughter.

Illustrations

Plate 1. Francesco del Cossa, *April* (fresco, Ferrara, Palazzo Schifanoia)

Plate 2. Detail of Pl. 1.

Plate 3. Girolamo da Carpi, *Venus on the Eridanus* (Dresden, Staatliche Gemäldegalerie)

Plate 4. Workshop of Meidias, *Aphrodite Anadyomene* (vase; after *Jahrbuch des Kaiserlich Deutschen Archäologischen Instituts,* I [Berlin, 1887], Tafel 11, no. 2)

Plate 5. *Venus on a Shell* (terra cotta figurine, Paris, Musée du Louvre)

Plate 6. Sandro Botticelli, *The Birth of Venus* (Florence, Uffizi)

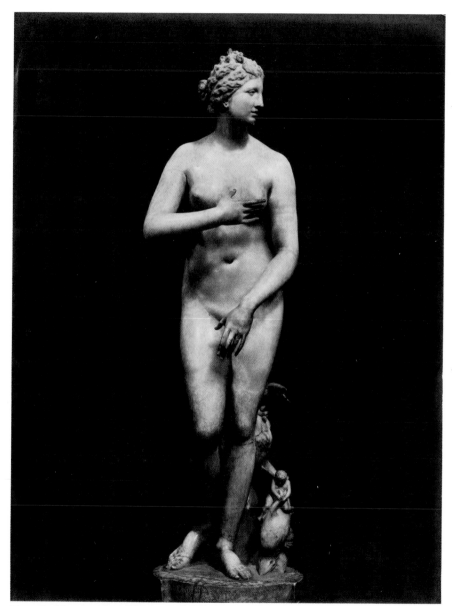

Plate 7. *Venus pudica* (Florence, Uffizi)

Plate 8. Titian, *Venus and the Lute Player* (New York, The Metropolitan Museum of Art, Munsey Fund, 1936)

Plate 9. Hans Mielich, *Cipriano de Rore* (Munich, Bayerische Staatsbibliothek, Mus. Ms. B, fol. 149)

Plate 10. Girolamo da Carpi, *Portrait of a Gentleman (Girolamo Falletti)* (Rome, Galleria Nazionale di Palazzo Barberini)

Plate 11. Detail of Pl. 10

An Ancient Model of Falletti's Poem

Perhaps more famous than Apelles's painting of Aphrodite—lost, as all of Apelles's paintings[95]—are Praxiteles's sculptures of the Goddess of Love. Renaissance students of antiquity were acquainted with two famous statues of Aphrodite by Praxiteles, one draped, the other nude; "the nude one, after having been refused by the inhabitants of Kos, had become the glory of the Isle of Knidos."[96] The *Anthologia Graeca*, a famous collection of Greek poems from the seventh century B.C. to the tenth century A.D., printed in Florence in 1494, which nurtured whole generations of humanists, contains several poems on the Aphrodite of Knidos.[97] It is here that we find the models of Girolamo Falletti's poems on Anna d'Este, Carpi's Venus. A sample follows:

Paphian Cythera came through the sea to Knidos
    Wishing to see her own image.
Having gazed from every angle in that conspicuous space
    She cried: "Where did Praxiteles see me naked?"
Praxiteles did not see what was unlawful, but the iron
    Carved the Paphian just as Ares would have wanted her.[98]

In this ancient Greek poem we have an early testimony of Aphrodite's seeing a great sculptor's likeness of herself so deceptively similar that she cried out: "Where did Praxiteles see me naked?" The poet quickly denies that a mortal could have set eyes on a goddess in the state of nature and shifts the responsibility to another God, Ares, or Mars, as the Romans called him. Venus and Mars were lovers; when Vulcan, Venus's husband, discovered this, he made a fine transparent net designed to catch the lovers. The trick worked; the net tightened around Venus and Mars, and Vulcan, Hephaistos in Greek, the Olympian god of fire and metal work, called the gods together to enjoy the lovers' embarrassment. Never before had Olympus echoed to such hearty laughter. Venus and Mars are of course another favorite topic in Renaissance painting. But what is the meaning of the Greek poet's reference to Ares? He might have wished to suggest that Praxiteles was able to fashion so deceptive a likeness of Aphrodite's not because he saw her in the nude, but because her lover, the God of War, knew her form so well that he could, as it were, guide the artist's hands.

Falletti wrote not only Latin; he also translated from the Greek into Italian.[99] He could read the poem, which he probably used as a model, in the original Greek. All he had to do was to change Aphrodite to Venus, Knidos to Ferrara, Praxiteles the sculptor to Carpi the painter, and then interpose Anna d'Este as the painter's model for Venus. Of course, he added his own description of the goddess and rendered the whole scene more colorful and poignant.

Yet, this is not all that we find of ancient poetry in Rore's motet text. The poem ends with Venus's cry: "quid iuvat esse deam?" "What use is it to be a goddess?" These words are taken from Book XIII, line 965 of Ovid's *Metamorphoses*.[100] There Glaukus, formerly a simple fisherman, "is changed into a sea-divinity by his chance eating of a magic herb."[101] Unfortunately, he falls in love with Scylla, who is frightened by his monstrous figure, half man, half fish. He is heartbroken by her rejection and cries: "quid iuvat esse deum, si tu non tangeris istis?" "What profits it to be a god, if you [Scylla] are not moved by these things?"

The idea of Falletti's poem, then, was indebted to ancient Greek poetry. Its last words were taken from one of the best known works of a famous Roman poet.

Carpi's Portrait of Falletti

The bonds between Carpi and Falletti having been close, should we not surmise that Carpi rewarded the poet for celebrating him in elegant verses by painting a portrait of him? This is indeed a thought entertained by the earliest biographer of the painter, who believes the portrait shown in Pl. 10 to be of Falletti. Serafini gives as reason for this identification the weighty volumes on the desk that mark the gentleman as a writer, but he concedes the lack of decisive proof.[102] He overlooked, however, the evidence characteristic for the time and carefully planted by Carpi. Carpi's latest biographer, Amalia Mezzetti, as we shall see shortly, touched the door to the solution, but did not open it. Let us first study the attributes in the portrait in detail. There are the precious books bound in tooled leather and held together by leather clasps. This motif is continued at the right corner with a shelf full of books. The desk, in back of which the gentleman stands, carries an inkpot on a beautifully carved metal base, a goose quill, and a pair of scissors—the common tools of the writer; one sees them also in Quentin Metsijs's portrait of Erasmus.[103] But what do we see on the precious books, if we look hard? A cat—and the cat must be important, since it is allowed to sit on the books and the writer's hand is leaning on it (Pl. 11). Indeed, Mezzetti says that the cat probably points to the family, so far unknown, to which the gentleman belongs.[104] And she is right: but as is often the case, the solution to the mystery is too plain to be seen. The Latin word for cat is *feles, felis*. The best writers (Varro and Cicero[105]) spell the word *faelis* (nominative). The word is very close, especially in its preferred spelling, to "Falletti," which, in Italian, is a diminutive form. "Felino" is the Italian name for members of the cat family. I hope that art historians may henceforth accept Carpi's cat as Falletti's heraldic animal. They adopted Ernst Gombrich's idea that the wasps buzzing around Mars in Botticelli's *Mars and Venus*, in Italian called "vespe," were "the punning coat-of-arms of the Vespucci,"[106] although which Vespucci is still a matter of debate.[107]

Conclusion

There is perhaps a deeper meaning in the parable of Venus weeping before her image painted by a human hand. The goddess laments the loss of her uniqueness. Ages ago the gods had created Man. Now Man has achieved the ability to create godlike images. Prometheus had brought down the fire from the heavens and the mortals became craftsmen fashioning infinite numbers of things of use and beauty. Now however the craftsman has become a genius. For the first time in the history of civilization, Man felt he had learned to "create," something that only God could do.

"The medieval definition of creation was *creare ex nihilo*. St. Thomas Aquinas put it succinctly: 'To create means to produce something out of nothing.' From this premise the two conclusions follow logically that 'God alone creates' and 'no mortal being can create,' or in St. Thomas's terse Latin: *Solus Deus creat* and *Nullum corpus potest creare*. But St. Augustine had already maintained: *Creatura non potest creare.* "[108]

The Renaissance transferred "the epithet *divus*, applied in the Middle Ages only to saints, . . . to secular celebrities." Aretino spoke of "the divine Michelangelo." Sylvestro Ganassi, the Venetian, called Willaert *nuovo Prometheo della celeste Armonia* (*Regola Rubertina*, dedication to part II, 1543).[109]

It was the first genius of the Baroque, Monteverdi, who thought of Cipriano de Rore as *divino*.[110] Even the initiator of the Florentine Camerata and declared enemy of polyphonic music, Giovanni de' Bardi, made an exception for "the divine Cipriano," who, "straining every fibre of his genius, . . . devoted himself to making the verse and the sound of the words thoroughly intelligible in his madrigals,"[111] and he cited the following five-part madrigals: *Poichè m' invita amore* (1565), *Se bene il duolo* (1557), and *Di virtù, di costume, di valore* (1557).

Simonides, the ancient Greek poet of the sixth century (ca. 556–468 B.C.), is quoted by Plutarch as having said:

Painting is silent poetry
Poetry is speaking painting.[112]

In the Renaissance, music becomes more and more like poetry, poetry more and more like painting. The three are united in Rore's Venus motet as few other works of the Renaissance are. This single work of music shows the living tissue in which a composition of the Renaissance may be embedded. The court painter recreates the beauty of the princess in a picture of Venus; the court poet sings the praises of the princess and lauds the beauty of the painting; the court composer crowns the homage to the princess by setting the poet's verses to music. All of this illustrates the vibrant enthusiasm that this age felt for ancient Greek and Roman culture. It is this enthusiasm and the literature, philosophy, art, and music it created that is encompassed in the term *humanism,* from which we must not separate its deep roots in the newly experienced idea of *humanitas.*

Girolamo Falletti's Poems on Carpi's Venus Painting

The first edition of Falletti's poems appeared in the year 1546 with the title *Hieronymi Phalethi Savonensis Poematum Libri Septem. Apud Inclytam Ferrariam per Franciscum Rubeum. M.D.XLVI.*

The first of the seven books is dedicated to Ercole II and begins with a lengthy *laus musicae*, of which I quote the beginning:

Describant alii pugnas, atque inclyta regum
Facta canant, quibus ingentes in carmina vires.
Te te ego diva canam; tu (dum mihi vita manebit)
MUSICA sola meo semper celebrabere cantu.[1]

Others may recite the battles, and sing the magnificent
Deeds of kings that poetry has the power to magnify.
I shall sing of you, heavenly Goddess of Music,
Whilst breath remains in me. For you alone
Shall forever remain the theme of my verses.

Not only music is Falletti's theme, also art and in particular painting. The book contains no fewer than eleven poems on Carpi's Venus painting. This cycle is repeated in the edition of 1557. With a fine hand, Falletti revises the old poems, retouches the punctuation, and omits one of the old poems which he does not like any more. I quote and translate the ten poems in the revision of 1557;[2] I also add the unique poem of 1546 (see n. 5).

Fol. 88   In pictura[m] Annae Principis Estensis

Fingeret Estensem diam dum Carpius Annam,
    Sic reor huic tabulae est indita vita simul.
Hanc quoties specto, tunc me spectasse videtur,
    Et quamvis nequeat, dixeris ore loqui.

On the painting of Princess Anna d'Este

When Carpi painted the divine Anna d'Este,
 That painting, me seems, was at once endowed with life.
As often as I look at her, she seems to look at me,
 Yet, although she can't, one would say she was moving her lips in speech.

Fol. 88ᵛ   In eandem

Si spectas Annae ficta sub imagine formam,
 Eridani Nymphas, dixeris, Anna refert.
Quòd si non fictam, veram sed videris, inter
 Aetherias praestat, dixeris, Anna Deas.

To the same

If you see Anna's figure fashioned in the painting,
 You might say Anna resembles the nymphs of the Po.
But if you were to see her as real, not painted,
 You might say she is first among heaven's goddesses.

In eandem

Num Venus egreditur ponto, quam finxit Apelles?
 An ne ea, Praxitelis quae fabricata manu est?
Neutra quidem. Venerem sed si quis deneget esse,
 Divinum tamen hoc nemo negabit opus.

53

To the same

Is this Venus emerging from the sea, she whom Apelles painted?
  Or if not, is it the one whom the hand of Praxiteles molded?
Forsooth, she is neither. Yet, though some may deny that she be Venus,
  None will contest that this is a work divine.

In eandem

Anna suos picta dum cernit imagine vultus,
  Nescio quid tenui murmure visa loqui est.
Fallor, an hac picta lateo sub imagine, Carpi
  Vivus an hic docta spirat ab arte color?

To the same

As Anna beholds her features in the painted likeness,
  She seems to speak in a strange little murmur:
I wonder whether this is myself in the painting,
  Or whether here just living color bursts forth in Carpi's cunning art.

Ad Tabellam

Quae nuper rudis arbor eras,[3] nunc pulchra puellae
  Membra refers, debes hoc, reor, artifici.
Sed formosa tibi debet magis Anna, quòd illi
  Maxima de tabulis sit data fama tuis.

To the Painting

Once you were a wild tree; now you depict the beautiful limbs
    Of a maiden. This, I dare say, you owe to the painter.
But well-shaped Anna owes you much more:
    Your panels confer on her highest renown.

Fol. 89   Tabella loquitur

Anna ego sum, quid spectas? sim licet aspera tactu,
    Hos nequeas vultus credere forte meos.
Ne stupeas, si fallo homines: rex saepe Deorum
    Iuppiter, est factus bos, equus, imber, olor.

The Painting speaks

Anna I am, what do you look for? I may seem rough to the touch,
    Yet would you hardly distrust my countenance.
Be not astonished if I deceive the humans.[4] Even the King of the Gods,
    Jupiter, often appeared as a bull or a horse, a swan or a raincloud.

Ad Annam

Admirans Cytherea tuam sine labe figuram,
    Affigens terrae lumina, tristis ait.
O Dea, nec tecum vellem certare, sub ipso
    Causa licet Phrygio iudice nostra foret.

55

To Anna

As Venus admired your immaculate figure,
   Casting her eyes to the ground, sadly she said:
Oh Goddess, with you I would not wish to vie; let our
   Cause be submitted to the same Phrygian judge.[5]

Ad eandem

Hesperiae cum laeta suas inviseret urbes,
   Venit ad Eridani ditia regna Venus:
Et modo divitias miratur fertilis agri,
   Et modo Atestini moenia clara ducis.
Hic tum forte tuam vidit sub imagine formam,
   Et pictum in tabula noscere credit opus.
Quis mihi te similem pinxit mea dulcis imago?
   Sola meos vultus quàm bene picta refers.
Vera mei effigies, ait, est hic vultus, et ipsum
   Pectus, et os, eadem lumina, labra, manus.
Ut vero Eridani Nympham te agnovit, obortis
   Sic fata est lacrymis, quid iuvat esse Deam?

See pages 7 and 32–34 for translation.

56

Ad eandem

Egreditur Cytherea mari, quis pinget Apelles?
    Quis canet hanc docto carmine Moeonides?
Inveni. Carpensis erit qui pinget Apelles;
    Et qui laude feret Pyrrhus, Homerus erit.

To the same

Venus comes out from the sea; which Apelles will paint her?
    Which Homer will praise her in erudite verse?
I know. Carpi will be the Apelles to paint her;
    And Pyrrhus[6] the Homer who will sing her praises.

Ad eandem

Luserat hanc tenui dominam nova dextera cedro,
    Phidiacha melior Praxitelisque manu.
Sed fragilis nimium & cuicunque obnoxia fato
    Infelix poterat mille pericla pati.
Non tulit hanc pollens musis & Apolline sortem
    Saraccus, docto carmine sanxit opus.

To the same

A new artist [*dextera*] had recast this lady in thin cedar wood,
  Better than Phidias and Praxiteles.
However, it was too fragile and exposed to any accident.
  Precarious, it could suffer a thousand perils.
Saraccus, made strong through Apollo and the Muses, did not tolerate this chance;
  He rendered the work inviolable through an erudite poem.

With great tact Falletti arranged his poems so that both the painter and the princely model could be satisfied. The introductory poem names Carpi and Anna together in the first line. Praising the artist for the life–like quality of the painting—a criterion characteristic for the Renaissance in general—he concedes that there was one thing he could not do: he could not make her speak, implying—what we expect to be true of a lady fluent in several languages—that Anna was an attractive speaker and that there were aspects of her the finest painter could not reproduce.

The second poem dedicated to Anna elevates her from the rank of the nymphs of the Eridanus to the goddesses of Olympus. The third one approximates her to Venus and compensates Carpi by declaring his work to be divine. Number four has Anna wondering whether it is herself that she sees or just an outburst of living color from Carpi's clever hand. Again the poet strikes a balance between painter and model. The fifth poem is addressed to the painting done on wood, reminding it of having once been but a wild tree, whereas now it shows the beauty of a young woman. However beautiful Anna is, she owes her fame to Carpi. In the next poem the painting is made to speak and reaffirms what its predecessor had said; its wooden panels may seem rough to the touch, but now wood is transformed into a beauty so ravishing that people think her Venus. Jupiter too deceived the humans, appearing in various forms to them. The seventh poem has Venus herself admire Anna's figure, declining to enter into a contest with her, leaving the matter rather in the hands of a Phrygian judge far away.

Number eight sings of the previously reported story of Venus's journey through Italy and her discovery of her likeness in Carpi's painting. Again Carpi and Anna receive evenhanded acclaim. In the ninth poem the question is raised who the modern Apelles is to paint Venus and who the modern Homer to chant her praises. Carpi shall be today's Apelles and, with astonishing modesty, the poet, being Falletti, names his friend Pyrrhus (Diego Pires) as the modern Homer—a not quite comprehensible compliment, since we have not met with a poem from Pyrrhus Didacus's pen on Carpi's painting (which does not mean that none exists).[7]

The tenth poem introduces (Battista) Saraccus, Secretary of Ercole II and Prefect of his archives, whose name occurs in Falletti's poems of 1557 both as addressee of the author and addressing him.[8] I regret not to be able to furnish information about a Venus statue made of cedar wood or to explain how a poem can render a delicate statue infrangible, except as a form of flattery.

In Falletti's cycle of poems we have direct contemporary testimony from a court poet of Ferrara on Carpi's authorship of *Venus on the Eridanus*. This is a powerful argument against Felton Gibbons's theory, based on his stylistic analysis, that Dosso Dossi played an important part in this painting.[9] Since Dosso Dossi also worked at the court of Ferrara, it is unthinkable that he would not have been mentioned by Falletti, had he indeed played the important role in the creation of this painting assigned to him by Gibbons.

There exists yet another poem on a painting of Anna d'Este by Carpi, written by the Ferrarese historian of literature, Lilio Gregorio Giraldi.[10] It is published in *Tomus Secundus* of the complete edition:

Estensis quota pars decoris Annae
Haec est, nam reliquas nitentiores,
Queis natura nihil iuvatur arte,
Pictoris manus haud potest referre.

59

Ipsam si videas, putabis unam,
Quicquid Pierides novem sorores,
Quicquid tres charites, simul tenere,
Et Pallas sine Gorgonis colubris.
Quare haec tantula pars nitoris Annae
Quae carpi potuit manu reponi.

Whatever part of beauteous Anna d'Este
This is—the others being even more sublime—
And here can Art not supersede the work of Nature;
No painter's hand can do it slightest justice.
Were you to see her, you would think she does combine
In one the Pierian Muses, nine in all,
Three Graces and Pallas Athena too
(Minus the snaky locks of Gorgons' heads).
Hence can you see of Anna's beauty only
What could be reproduced by Carpi's hand.[11]

Giraldi heaps all praise on Anna; Carpi is played down to the point of depriving his name of its initial capital.

Giraldi introduces his poem with an account of his conversation with Antonius Antimachus and Bartholomeus Riccius:

We fell to talking about the wedding, which was then being celebrated, of Anna d'Este, daughter of our princes, the most attractive young woman, endowed with every virtue and all the elegance worthy of a princess. The rare gifts of body and mind of this illustrious young lady I could not celebrate more concisely than in these eleven-syllable verses which I had composed on her picture done by our painter Carpi some months ago.[12]

The date for Carpi's painting as done "superioribus mensibus" and the mention of the wedding, which took place in 1548, suggest that the likeness of Anna was not *Venus on the Eridanus* but one of Carpi's portraits of the Este children sent to the Queen of France at the end of 1547. The Queen's Master of Ceremonies wrote Ercole II on the third of January, 1548, thanking him in the queen's name for the portraits of all the children of the Este family[13] sent to Primaticcio (who then worked in France) to present to her. She and the whole court had enjoyed and admired them.

It is probably Anna's portrait from this series that Falletti praises in these two distichs:

In picturam Principis Atestinae

Talis est facies, habitus quoque, talis et Annae
    Maiestas, color & talis in ore nitor.

On the portrait of the Princess d'Este

Such is her face and this her appearance, and such is Anna's
    Splendor, the very color and radiance of her features.

Aliud

Spirantes Annae si cernis imagine vultus,
    Dices, sic oculos, sic caput Anna movet.[14]

Another one

If you see Anna's life-like features in the painting,
    You will say, yes, so does Anna move her eyes and so her head.

Endnotes

1. Edith Hamilton, *Mythology* (Boston, 1942), p. 33.

2. Not that Venus's life was free of tears. From Ovid's *Metamorphoses* we learn of her sorrows: Adonis prefers the hunt to her love and dies when attacked by a boar; Caesar, descendant of her son Aeneas, is to be murdered and Jupiter tells her that no one can go against the Fates; *Ovid, the Metamorphoses*, trans. Horace Gregory (New York, 1958), pp. 289–90 and 437–41. On Caesar's descendancy from Venus, see Robert Schilling, *La Religion romaine de Vénus depuis les origines jusqu'au temps d'Auguste* (Paris, 1954), pp. 301ff.

3. *Cipriani Rore Opera omnia*, I, ed. Bernhard Meier, Corpus Mensurabilis Musicae, XIV (n.p.: American Institute of Musicology, 1959), pp. 127–32.

4. The first great characterization of Rore, the madrigalist, was given by Alfred Einstein in his three-volume work, *The Italian Madrigal* (Princeton, 1949), I, 384–423.

5. See Gustave Gruyer, *L'Art ferrarais à l'époque des princes d'Este*, 2 vols. (Paris, 1897), I, 374–77.

6. The monumental work of Gruyer, *L'Art ferrarais à l'époque des princes d'Este*, still gives the best general survey of Ferrarese art and art patronage under the Este family. See also the recent compact, yet comprehensive study by Werner L. Gundersheimer on *Ferrara, The Style of a Renaissance Despotism* (Princeton, 1973), esp. chapter VII, "Courtly Style in the Visual Arts," pp. 229–71.

7. For a painting by Titian commissioned by Duke Alfonso I (1505–34), see Lowinsky, "Music in Titian's *Bacchanal of the Andrians*: Origin and History of the *Canon per tonos*," in *Titian. His World and His Legacy*, ed. David Rosand, Bampton Lectures in America, XXI (New York, 1982), pp. 191–282.

8. On the history of the palace and its frescoes, see Gruyer, *L'Art ferrarais*, I, 419–68.

9. A. Warburg, "Italienische Kunst und internationale Astrologie im Palazzo Schifanoja zu Ferrara," *Gesammelte Schriften*, 2 vols. (Leipzig-Berlin, 1932), II, 459–81; see p. 463: "Jedes Monatsbild besteht aus drei parallel übereinander angeordneten Bildflächen mit selbständigem

Bildraum und etwa halblebensgrossen Figuren. Auf deren obersten Fläche ziehen die olympischen Götter auf Triumphwagen einher, unten wird das irdische Treiben am Hofe des Herzogs Borso erzählt; . . . der mittlere Streifen gehört der astralen Götterwelt."

The reader should be warned that so great an authority as E. H. Gombrich, in his work *Aby Warburg, An Intellectual Biography* (London, 1970), pp. 312–13, calls it "a travesty . . . to connect Warburg with this branch of art history. . . . For Warburg iconography was marginal. . . . If Warburg turned to iconography it was in fact only to make this paedagogic point." If Gombrich is right—and I suspect that a number of art historians would differ with him—then it is possible for a non-iconographer to be the father of modern iconography. Gombrich himself, in a few brilliant pages (315–17), showed that Fritz Saxl and Erwin Panofsky were the dedicated and successful followers of Warburg. These two scholars are remembered by him for their joint work on Dürer's *Melencolia* (*Studien der Bibliothek Warburg*, II; Leipzig and Berlin, 1923), and Gombrich feels constrained to say that this study "was to prove the viability of *Warburg's type of iconology*" (p. 317; emphasis added).

10. The frescoes are the work of a number of painters. Cossa's authorship for the frescoes dedicated to the month of April is established in the artist's petition of 25 March 1470 to Duke Borso in which he asks not to be paid for his work as if he were one of the lowliest apprentices. For the Italian text of the unusual petition, see A. Venturi, who discovered and published it in *Der Kunstfreund* (1 May 1885, no. 9); it is also given in Eberhard Ruhmer, *Francesco del Cossa* (Munich, 1959), p. 48; for a French translation of the document, see Gruyer, *L'Art ferrarais*, I, 447–48. Werner Gundersheimer, in his book on Ferrara, p. 171, refers to Cossa's letter and adds: "Whether Borso responded to Cossa's pleas with the 'Iustitia' upon which he prided himself, and under the sign of which he had himself shown in those very same frescoes [see Gruyer, *L'Art ferrarais*, I, 430], we do not know." Borso's negative, curt response has been noted by Gruyer, *L'Art ferrarais*, I, 448, and Ruhmer, *Cossa*, p. 49. Gundersheimer's question whether the answer reflects "Iustitia" can be answered in the negative and the positive according to the definition of "justice."

If we expect the prince to form an independent judgment, the answer must be "no"; if the term is confined to the duke's making sure that the matter had gone through the official channels, then the answer is "yes." That Cossa was of the former opinion, we may deduce from his reaction to Borso's answer: he moved to Bologna where he stayed until his death, honored and successful.

11. The philosophical foundation for this and similar Italian paintings is Plato's idea that "Love is more powerful than strife" (*Symposium* 196D), supported also by Lucretius, in his "famous invocation of Venus against Mars" (*De rerum natura*, I, 30–41) cited by Edgar Wind, *Pagan Mysteries in the Renaissance* (New Haven, 1958), p. 84, n. 1.

Neither Warburg nor Wind have paid much attention to the non–pagan figures. They appear to be Ferrarese courtiers, obviously under the influence of Venus, and they interest us for their relationship to music; see below, pp. 26–27. (For a detail of this section of the fresco, see Lewis Lockwood, "Music at Ferrara in the Period of Ercole I d'Este," *Studi musicali*, I [1972], 101–31; opposite p. 110.)

12. Alberto Serafini, *Girolamo da Carpi, pittore e architetto ferrarese (1501–1556)* (Rome, 1915), p. 91.

13. Felton Gibbons, *Dosso and Battista Dossi, Court Painters at Ferrara* (Princeton, 1968), p. 223.

14. *Ibid.*

15. Erwin Panofsky, *Renaissance and Renascences in Western Art* (Stockholm, 1960), p. 197. See also below, note 24.

16. In fact, there is evidence that the painting was known under this title at the time of its origin; see below, note 93.

17. A. Pigler, in his monumental work *Barockthemen*, 2 vols. (Budapest and Berlin, 1956), II, 147–51, lists over 120 art works depicting "Leda mit dem Schwan," of which fewer than half belong to the sixteenth, more than half to the seventeenth and eighteenth centuries. He cites not a single reference to Venus and the swans for these later centuries.

18. I realize that I am out of my depth in a field not my speciality; I intend to do no more than raise a few careful queries. Gibbons himself is very cautious; he does not consider his thoughts as well-established facts. On the contrary, he observes: "At this writing the painting awaits a more thorough laboratory examination which will reveal the full extent of these alterations and perhaps clarify the confused history and iconography of the work, as well as the problem of its dual ascription" (*Dosso and Battista Dossi*, p. 223).

19. Hamilton, *Mythology*, p. 33.

20. See A. Kalkmann, "Aphrodite auf dem Schwan," *Jahrbuch des kaiserlich deutschen Archäologischen Instituts,* I (1886), 231–60, Tafel 11, 2. For further literary and artistic references to Venus and the swan, see Guy de Tervarent, *Attributs et symboles dans l'art profane 1450–1600* (Geneva, 1959), col. 81: Char traîné par des cygnes, I. Le Char de Vénus. For a multiplicity of other symbolic uses, see also "Cygne," cols. 138–41.

21. See Joseph Clark Hoppin, *A Handbook of Attic Red-Figured Vases,* 3 vols. (Washington, D.C., 1973), II, 177. For its present location, see II, 195 (Berlin 2688). For further literature, see both passages. A brief survey of Greek vase-painting from the ninth to the third centuries can be found in *The Oxford Classical Dictionary* (Oxford, 1961), p. 938, article "Vase-Painting."

22. See Norman W. Canedy, *The Roman Sketchbook of Girolamo da Carpi,* Studies of the Warburg Institute, XXXV, ed. E. H. Gombrich (London, 1976). In her review of Canedy's book (*Renaissance Quarterly,* XXXII [1979], 391–93; p. 392), Diane DeGrazia Bohlin writes: "he has not shown in any cases conclusively that Girolamo's drawings after the antique were definitely after later copies."

23. Paul Jamot, "Vénus à la coquille. Deux figurines de terre cuite. Musée du Louvre," *Monuments et Mémoires publiés par l'Académie des Inscriptions et Belles-Lettres,* II (Paris, 1895), 171–84.

24. Botticelli's painting has been seen universally as "The Birth of Venus." His latest biographer, Ronald Lightbown, takes issue with this interpretation: "In reality the subject of the

picture is not the birth of Venus . . . , but Venus landing on the shore after her birth"; *Sandro Botticelli*, 2 vols. (Berkeley and Los Angeles, 1978), I, 88–89. That birth and landing could be considered one and the same subject by one of the painter's contemporaries—taking the word in its broadest meaning—may be seen from the description of Giorgio Vasari, who, in his history of Italian painting, writes: "At Castello, a villa of Duke Cosimo, there are two narrative pictures: one showing Venus as she is born and those breezes and winds that bring her ashore, together with the Cupids; and also another Venus whom the Graces adorn with flowers, denoting Spring"; *Le Vite de' più eccellenti pittori scultori ed architettori scritte da Giorgio Vasari pittore Aretino*, ed. with commentaries by Gaetano Milanesi, 9 vols. (Florence, 1906), III, 312, quoted by Panofsky, *Renaissance and Renascences*, p. 197. (The first edition of Vasari's *Vite* was published in 1550, the second in 1568.) Vasari's description would also seem to differ from Lightbown's statement (I, 88) that "the *Birth of Venus* is a title first given it in the nineteenth century," unless one takes the word "title" in its narrowest sense. The second painting, known under the name that Vasari gave it, "Primavera," shows a Venus fully, if transparently, dressed. The painting, interpreted generally as a *Garden of Venus* (Lightbown, *Botticelli*, I, 74), has usually been taken together by art historians with Botticelli's *Birth of Venus*. Panofsky sees in the two paintings the personifications of the "celestial" and the "terrestrial" Venus, a distinction that goes back to Plato's *Symposium* and was developed by Botticelli's fellow citizen Marsilio Ficino in his commentary on the *Symposium* (*Problems in Titian, Mostly Iconographic* [New York, 1969], p. 114; for an extended discussion of Botticelli's *Venus* and *Primavera*, see *idem, Renaissance and Renascences*, pp. 192–200).

25. Panofsky, *Problems in Titian*, p. 112.

26. Lightbown, *Botticelli*, I, ill. 49; also E. H. Gombrich, "Botticelli's Mythologies," ill. 35 (see note 34 below).

27. Norman W. Canedy starts the preface to his publication of *The Roman Sketchbook of Girolamo da Carpi* with the words: "This study of a Mannerist artist's Roman sketchbook. . . ."

The most penetrating stylistic study of Carpi came from the pen of F. Antal in his paper

"Observations on Girolamo da Carpi," *The Art Bulletin*, XXX (1948), 81–103. Placing the painter into the full context of his time, artistically, culturally, socially, he defines his position in Italian painting as between classicism and mannerism. He stresses Ercole II's preference for mannerists, whenever he called for painters outside Ferrara; Pordenone and Giulio Romano are outstanding examples.

See also Lowinsky, "The Problem of Mannerism in Music: An Attempt at a Definition," *Studi musicali*, III (1974; publ. 1977), 131–218; see esp. pp. 134–40: "An Art Historical Definition of Mannerism," dealing with Gombrich's critical attitude toward the concept. The paper distances itself from the tendency of art historians to apply the term "mannerism" to the whole pre-Baroque era.

28. *Botticelli*, I, 89.

29. Margarete Bieber, *Ancient Copies. Contributions to the History of Greek and Roman Art* (New York, 1977), p. 65.

30. See A. Michaelis, "Zur Geschichte des Schleifers in Florenz und der Mediceischen Venus," *Archäologische Zeitung*, XXXVIII (1880), 11–17.

31. W. S. Heckscher, "The *Anadyomene* in the Medieval Tradition (Pelagia–Cleopatra–Aphrodite). A Prelude to Botticelli's 'Birth of Venus,'" *Netherlands Year-Book for History of Art* (1956), pp. 1–38. The study furnishes, as the title suggests, a history of Venus in the medieval tradition.

32. Lightbown, *Botticelli*, II, C10, 11, 12 on p. 121.

33. A. Warburg, *Gesammelte Schriften*, I, 6–22: "Sandro Botticelli's 'Geburt der Venus' und 'Frühling' [Primavera], Erster Abschnitt, 'Die Geburt der Venus.'"

34. E. H. Gombrich, "Botticelli's Mythologies: A Study in the Neo-Platonic Symbolism of his Circle," *Journal of the Warburg and Courtauld Institutes*, VIII (1945), 7–60. I refer to the revised edition of this essay in *Symbolic Images. Studies in the Art of the Renaissance* (New York, 1972), pp. 31–81.

35. *Botticelli*, II, 64.

36. Antal, ". . . Girolamo da Carpi," p. 83.

37. A description of the five main Venus presentations and their repeats and copies can be found in Harold E. Wethey, *The Paintings of Titian*, 3 vols. (London, 1969–75), III, 63–70; see plates 105 (Prado), 113 (Prado), 114 (Berlin), 122 (New York), 123 (Cambridge). See also Panofsky's fascinating discussion in *Problems in Titian*, pp. 121–25.

38. Otto Brendel, "The Interpretation of the Holkham *Venus*," *The Art Bulletin*, XXVIII (1946), 65–75; p. 66.

39. Not even Emanuel Winternitz, who takes generous notice of Brendel's study, disputes his interpretation; see "The Knowledge of Musical Instruments as an Aid to the Art Historian," in *Musical Instruments and Their Symbolism in Western Art* (New Haven and London, 1979), pp. 52–53.

40. Later in the article, Brendel does mention the two musical instruments; see below.

41. The sixteenth century had a large repertory of instrumental duets in print; see Howard Mayer Brown, *Instrumental Music Printed before 1600, A Bibliography* (Cambridge, Mass., 1965), p. 478, under "Ensemble *a 2* for instruments." But the lute is of course a harmonic instrument and Venus, playing the recorder to the lute's accompaniment, could have performed any chanson or madrigal of the period.

42. A convenient reproduction appears in the article on "Liszt" in *The New Grove Dictionary of Music and Musicians*, XI, 37.

43. Brendel, "The Interpretation," p. 66.

44. Titian also noted the swans on Cossa's fresco, attributes of Venus that pull the throne on which the two gods are riding, for they reappear in "Venus and the Lutenist," swimming in the water to the left side.

45. Wethey, *Paintings of Titian*, III, 67.

46. *Ibid.*, pl. 123; discussion on pp. 66–67.

47. David Rosand, *Titian* (New York, 1978), p. 36.

48. See below, pp. 42–43.

49. Wethey, *Paintings of Titian*, III, 67.

50. E. H. Gombrich, "Botticelli's Mythologies," p. 47. (Neither Wethey nor Gombrich were interested in an association between Venus and the flute.) Frequent occurrence of the flute in paintings of Venus and those born under her planet ("the children of Venus") can be found in the study of A. P. de Mirimonde, "La musique dans les allégories de l'amour," *Gazette des Beaux-Arts*, LXVIII (1966), 265–90. The article covers the period from the fifteenth to the eighteenth centuries. The same subject transposed to a lower social stratum is treated by H. Colin Slim in the University of California Distinguished Lecture of 1975–76, "The Prodigal Son at the Whores'. Music, Art, and Drama." Slim deals with the "numerous cycles of woodcuts and engravings, particularly in the Low Countries and in Germany," on the subject during the sixteenth century. His paper shows many illustrations with scenes depicting musicians with instruments, a number of them flutes played by young women; it is especially valuable because Slim succeeds in identifying in several instances the music from which the musicians play.

51. Winternitz, "The Knowledge of Musical Instruments," p. 53.

52. *Ibid.*, p. 48.

53. *Ibid.*, pp. 49–50.

54. Brendel, "The Interpretation," p. 74.

55. *Ibid.* On the *paysage moralisée*, see Erwin Panofsky, *Studies in Iconology* (New York, 1962), p. 64.

56. Lockwood, *Music in Renaissance Ferrara 1400–1505* (Cambridge, Mass., 1984), p. 91.

57. See *Ottaviano Petrucci, Canti B*, ed. Helen Hewitt, Monuments of Renaissance Music, II, gen. ed. Edward E. Lowinsky (Chicago, 1967), plate VII.

58. *Johannis Pierii Valeriani . . . Hieroglyphica* (Cologne, 1614), p. 666; see Ulrich Middeldorf, Letter to the Editor on Brendel's essay, *The Art Bulletin*, XXIX (1947), 65–67; 66b.

59. Panofsky, *Studies in Iconology*, pp. 163–64; *idem, Problems in Titian*, p. 127.

60. See Egon Verheyen, *The Paintings in the* Studiolo *of Isabella d'Este at Mantua* (New York, 1971), p. 38, n. 70.

61. Edgar Wind, *Pagan Mysteries in the Renaissance*, p. 123, n. 1. Wind refers to Erasmus but omits saying that Erasmus makes Augustine responsible for the statement.

62. See B. Jowett, *The Dialogues of Plato*, 4 vols., 4th ed. (Oxford, 1953), I, 519 (187c). In book VIII, ch. 2 of his *De civitate Dei*, Augustine speaks of Socrates' disciples and says: "Inter discipulos Socratis, non quidem immerito, excellentissima gloria claruit, quae omnino caeteros obscuraret, Plato"; see *Friedrich Ueberwegs Grundriss der Geschichte der Philosophie, Zweiter Teil. Die Patristische und Scholastische Philosophie*, ed. Bernhard Geyer, 12th ed. (Basel, 1951), pp. 102–3.

63. *Confessions*, X, Ch. 33. For the whole passage, see Donald Jay Grout, *A History of Western Music*, rev. ed. (New York, 1973), p. 26. See also Lowinsky, "The Music in 'St. Jerome's Study,'" an epilogue to Helen I. Roberts, "St. Augustine in 'St. Jerome's Study': Carpaccio's Painting and Its Legendary Source," *The Art Bulletin*, XLI (1959), 283–301; 298–301. For a penetrating and well-documented study of the evolution of St. Augustine's ideas on music, see Heinrich Hüschen's article in *Die Musik in Geschichte und Gegenwart*, I (1949–51), cols. 848–57.

64. Lowinsky, *Das Antwerpener Motettenbuch Orlando di Lasso's und seine Beziehungen zum Motettenschaffen der niederländischen Zeitgenossen* (The Hague, 1937), pp. 80–81.

65. In his capacity as Ferrarese ambassador to Venice, Falletti, in 1558, became involved in a controversy surrounding a projected unauthorized publication by a Venetian nobleman of four of Willaert's madrigals from the *Musica nova*, then in process of publication under the editorship of Francesco della Viola and sponsorship of Prince Alfonso d'Este, who had obtained the collection from the famed Venetian singer Polisena Pecorina, a favorite of Willaert's, in 1554. Falletti appealed to the Venetian Senate and obtained from the Doge an order that the four madrigals could not appear in print before della Viola's ten-year privilege had expired. The affair dragged on until the end of February 1559, when Falletti finally succeeded in reaching the necessary

agreements. For documentation of the controversy, which involved Alfonso's secretary Giovanni Battista Pigna and Duke Ercole as well, see Anthony Newcomb, "Editions of Willaert's *Musica nova*: New Evidence, New Speculations," *Journal of the American Musicological Society*, XXVI (1973), 132–45; 137–40.

66. Paolo Manuzio, son of the famed Venetian printer Aldo Manuzio (1450–1515), brought out an expanded and revised edition of these poems in the year 1557 under the title *Hieronymi Faleti De bello Sicambrico Libri IIII. Et eiusdem alia poemata libri VIII* (see Excursus).

67. She gave refuge to French Protestants. In 1535 Clément Marot escaped to her court and was made her secretary. In 1536 John Calvin, the Reformer, spent two months in Ferrara; see Bartolommeo Fontana, "Documenti dell'Archivio Vaticano e dell'Estense circa il soggiorno di Calvino a Ferrara," *Archivio della R. Società Romana di Storia Patria*, VIII (1885), 101–39. In that same year the duke, under papal pressure, exiled all Protestants from Ferrara. A brief description of Renée's court can be found in Luciano Chiappini's book on *Gli Estensi* (Varese, 1967), pp. 253ff. For a life of Renée, see Bartolommeo Fontana, *Renata di Francia, duchessa di Ferrara*, 3 vols. (Rome, 1889–99), and E. Rodocanachi, *Renée de France* (Paris, 1896).

68. Angelo Solerti and Giuseppe Campori, *Luigi, Lucrezia e Leonora d'Este* (Turin, 1888), p. 30, n. 2, and A. Solerti, *Ferrara e la Corte Estense nella seconda metà del secolo decimosesto* (Città di Castello, 1900), p. CXVI, assumed that "Milleville, chantre" referred to Alessandro. Anthony Newcomb, in his article on the Milleville family of musicians in *The New Grove Dictionary of Music and Musicians*, XII, 323, considers it likely that the music teacher of the princesses was Alessandro's father Jean, who served at the court of Renée de France since at least 1534.

69. Serafini, *Girolamo da Carpi*, p. 124.

70. Amalia Mezzetti, in her book, *Girolamo da Ferrara detto da Carpi, L'Opera pittorica* (Milan, 1977), p. 58, refers to an account dated 26 January 1544 in which Carpi is being paid the sum of sixteen scudi for the *Venus on the river Po* (cited there under a byname, *La Galatea*); see note 93 below. Falletti's poem was published in 1546.

71. Rore is first recorded at Ferrara in May 1546; see Jessie Ann Owens, "The Milan Partbooks: Evidence of Cipriano de Rore's Compositional Process," *Journal of the American Musicological Society*, XXXVII (1984), 270–98; see p. 278, n. 13. I believe that he may have arrived in Ferrara as early as 1545, which may have been the date for his Venus motet.

In a recent article, Richard J. Agee presents four letters to Ruberto Strozzi in which Cipriano de Rore is mentioned, one of 1541 (?), one of 1545, and two of 1546 ("Ruberto Strozzi and the Early Madrigal," *Journal of the American Musicological Society*, XXXVI [1983], 1–17). The author attempts to deduce from these letters some biographic data for the early career of Cipriano. He says with regard to the first letter: "The letter printed above seems to show Rore in Venice as early as 1541" (p. 14). This conclusion, however cautiously phrased, does not follow from the evidence, for the author assigns this letter not to "1541" but to "1541?" The letter is part of "a *busta* of correspondence dated from 1540 to 1544" (p. 12, n. 39). Agee dated the letter first as of 1540, then 1541 without giving any reasons for his change of mind. Unfortunately, no facsimile is provided to enable the reader to make up his own mind. If a zero can be read as "1," then the letter might just as well be assigned to the years 1542, 1543, or 1544. And since the following letters carry the dates of 1545 and 1546 and they all deal with the same issue, i.e. how to procure music of Cipriano de Rore, a date of 1544 would make more sense than one of 1541.

In the second letter, dated Fano, 16 April 1545, Pallazzo da Fano writes to Ruberto Strozzi that he is sending "some music of Cipriano's and when I'm in Brescia I will send you the newest things" (p. 14). Agee's deduction as to Cipriano's stay in Brescia at that time is likewise no more than speculative; it is a possibility, by no means a certainty. Brescia was a brilliant center of music in the sixteenth century and there may have been a number of musicians from whom Pallazzo could have obtained the most recent works of Rore. If the composer was so much sought after by connoisseurs like the Strozzis, it is unlikely that no document would survive showing him in Brescia, if he really resided there at that time. All the same, Richard Agee deserves credit for his discovery of these letters in the inexhaustible archives of the city of Florence.

72. Falletti writes "pictura"; in a later edition, the *Delitiae CC. Italorum Poetarum . . . collectore Ranutio Ghero* [Janus Gruterus], 2 vols. (Frankfurt, 1608), I, 947, the more common reading "in picturam" is adopted.

73. "Hinc," in the 1546 reading, must be a misprint; it makes no sense.

74. In the discussion following my paper at the Annual Meeting of the American Musicological Society in Philadelphia (1984), Jessie Ann Owens mentioned that the version of Rore's motet in MS Wolfenbüttel 293 includes the name Anna, which she thought would solve the problem for which I had no answer, namely, why the text of Rore's motet, as given by Gardane in 1549, had eliminated Falletti's references to Anna. MS Wolfenbüttel 293 indeed has Anna's name, not where Falletti's poem has it but as a substitute ("annę") for the word "amnis" (in the phrase from mm. 35 to 41). The answer to the question, however, hinges on the authority of the sources: which one represents Rore's original text? This problem has not yet been solved.

At the same meeting Mary S. Lewis read a paper dealing with Rore's *Vergine bella* cycle and the role of the Wolfenbüttel manuscript in the history of its transmission. In her handout she quoted, in a valuable table (8), "unique text variants outside 'Vergine bella' in Wolf 293." She drew attention to four variant readings for *Hesperiae cum laeta* in the Wolfenbüttel manuscript, one of which is "annę"; the others are "agro" (instead of *agri* in mm. 24–28), "dulcis" (instead of *ducis* in alto and tenor of mm. 33–35), "vidit" (instead of *credit* in the quintus of m. 50). To these can be added "inviscerat" (instead of *inviserat*, in the alto, tenor, and quintus, mm. 4–10), "mirantur" (instead of *miratur*, tenor, m. 25), "lumine" (instead of *lumina* in mm. 91–93), "ob ortis" (instead of *obortis* in mm. 106–9). All of these would more precisely be characterized as erroneous rather than variant readings. Indeed, one may wonder whether anyone who can write "inviscerat" instead of "inviserat," "eadem lumine" instead of "lumina," "ob ortis" instead of "obortis" knows Latin.

There is another category of divergences that may go under the name of variants, and these are variant spellings: *Hesperie quum leta* instead of *Hesperiae cum laeta*, *ymago* instead of *imago*, *lachrimis* instead of *lachrymis*. But it is impossible to draw any conclusions from this at an age where variety in spellings is a universal practice and appreciated more as a virtue than condemned as a vice. Several of Wolfenbüttel's variants are also found in Paris, Bibliothèque nationale, MS Rés. 1591, no. 3: *Hesperie quum leta, annae, lumine, ob ortis,* and *mirantur* in the tenor, indicating that they may have been copied from a common source, or one from the other, if the scribe was able to correct the obvious errors. Curiously, two of these readings are also found in the Scotto print of Rore's motets, which came out in the same year as Gardane's (RISM 1549[7]): *Hesperie quum leta* and *lumine*. But Scotto gives *amnis* instead of *anne*. The Quintus reads *inviseret,* following Falletti's version of the poem, but the Bassus has *inviserat*. Scotto spells *Eridani* both as *Aeridani* and *Eridani* and introduces an erroneous *hac* instead of *hanc* in m. 99 (I have been able to check the Quinta pars and Bassus only). The Bourdeney manuscript (Paris, Bibliothèque nationale, MS Rés. Vma. 851, p. 54) agrees with Gardane except for a few minor variants (*ad* is missing in Superius, m. 14; Bassus, m. 27 has *fertiles* instead of *fertilis* and at mm. 41–43 reads *vidit pulchram*); it spells *lachrimis* and *nimpham* without a "y," except in the Superius at m. 109 and in the Tenor at m. 102, respectively. We hope that the comprehensive study that Mary S. Lewis is undertaking of the Wolfenbüttel manuscript will be capable of furnishing us with definitive answers to the question of its models. (It should be added that the manuscript consists of partbooks, of which the bass is missing.)

75. "E tutti questi particolari seppi io dallo stesso Girolamo, che fu molto mio amico, l'anno 1550, in Roma. . . . Fece anco non piccol danno a Girolamo nelle cose dell'arte l'avere atteso troppo a' suoi piaceri amorosi, ed a sonare il liuto in quel tempo che arebbe potuto fare acquisto nella pittura" (Vasari, *Le Vite,* ed. Milanesi, VI, 472–73). The motif of love and lute, love and music, has already been noted.

76. ". . . e si dilettò oltremodo della musica" (*ibid.,* 479).

77. Girolamo Baruffaldi, *Vite de' pittori e scultori ferraresi,* 2 vols. (Ferrara, 1844), I, 388 (Baruffaldi's dates are 1675–1755). Baruffaldi also writes about Carpi's collaboration with Alfonso della Viola in the performance of Cinthio Giovanni Battista Giraldi's tragedy *Orbecche* (I, 390; Cinthio was the nephew of Lilio Gregorio). For Cinthio's *Egle* the music was written by Antonio

dal Cornetto (I, 391). In his *Dialogo della musica* of 1544, Antonfrancesco Doni called the latter "il divino Antonio da Cornetto, perfettissimo" (Einstein, *The Italian Madrigal*, I, 197), and Baruffaldi praises him as a composer, comparing him in this capacity with Serafino dall'Aquila, although, he admits, no compositions of either survive.

78. ". . . hora havendo ritrovato questi miei parenti, dopoi la partita di là, per più disgratie accorsegli ruinati, si come haveva proposto di vivermi con loro in libertà e riposo, son sforzato tornare a nuovo giogho"; Edmond van der Straeten, *La Musique aux Pays-Bas avant le XIXe siècle*, 8 vols. (Brussels, 1867–88; repr. New York, 1969, with an Introduction by Edward E. Lowinsky), VI, 142. The letter is also published in Angelo Solerti, *Ferrara e la Corte Estense*, p. CXVII, n. 3, and in Josef Musiol, *Ciprian de Rore, ein Meister der venezianischen Schule* (Breslau, 1933), pp. 18–19.

79. See *The Italian Madrigal*, I, 386: ". . . it is not until November 12, 1559, that he assures Duke Alfonso, who in the meantime had succeeded his father Ercole, that he is ready at any time to return to the service of the Este family and that he will give preference to any offer from the Duke. But Alfonso, the eccentric patron of Torquato Tasso, turns a deaf ear for some unknown reason; perhaps because he did not fancy a certain phrase in Rore's letter: 'that he had hoped to be able to conclude his life in his homeland and near his parents, in liberty and quiet, but that their sad financial plight was now obliging him to bow to a fresh yoke' ('. . . son sforzato [di] tornare a nuovo giogo')."

When I put the finishing touches on this paper, it occurred to me I ought to read J. C. Hol's essay on "Cipriano de Rore" in *Festschrift. Karl Nef zum 60. Geburtstag* (Zürich, 1933), pp. 134–49, if for no other reason than Einstein's calling it "a little study, but by far the best thing written on Rore thus far" (*Italian Madrigal*, I, 389). What a surprise it was! Hol, the meritorious Orazio Vecchi scholar, whose name cannot be found in any of the great international dictionaries of music (except in the Vecchi and Rore bibliographies), has written the first striking portrait, albeit in form of a sketch, of Rore the man and the musician, and has written it in the hearty style of a Swiss. He started with the famous letter to Alfonso after the death of Ercole, and he concludes—I

77

translate—that it shows "how little Rore conformed to Castiglione's idea of the courtier, since he asks the new duke of Ferrara to restore him to his old office, but calls it a yoke that he will take up again with repugnance. This is the same Rore who cannot bring himself to dedicate even one of his works to a noble personality, as was the custom, for the sake of a return gift and protection that were the results of such a dedication. . . . He was a complete introvert who could not stand the hustle and intrigues of the metropolis Venice, and who compelled the doge personally to give him the leave refused him before to go back to Parma from where he never returned. He was happy to serve his former lord, who had a full appreciation of his merits, in leisure and quiet" (pp. 135–36).

Hol makes some small errors (he ascribes the first partial edition of the *Vergini* to Gardane instead of to Scotto; p. 138). But he has an unerring intuition for Rore's greatest works set to Italian texts. His examples are well chosen and intelligently discussed. He also utters a prophetic warning: "He who considers the work of a great master, but seeks only himself and the confirmation of his preconceived opinion, will eventually find not the master but only himself" (p. 149). And he closes with a profound thought: "It is not always true that 'the past is but a book with seven seals.' For him who loves there is no time, there is no past. There is only the omnipresence of human feeling" ("Es gibt nur die Allgegenwart des menschlichen Empfindens"; *ibid.*).

80. Alvin Johnson, author of the fundamental study on "The Liturgical Music of Cipriano de Rore" (Ph.D. dissertation, Yale University, 1954), missed the significance of the passage quoted above in his two articles on Rore in *Die Musik in Geschichte und Gegenwart* (XI, 1963, cols. 897–901) and *The New Grove* (XVI, 1980, 185–90), for he writes in the latter: "In July 1559 he again travelled to the north, determined to remain with his parents, but when he received news of Duke Ercole II's death on 3 October 1559 he immediately offered his services to Alfonso II, his successor. This proposal was refused, however . . ." (p. 186). All we can say is that it was ignored. Musiol too fails to come to grips with the meaning of this letter: ". . . probably the difficult circumstances of his parents continued, which spoiled his sojourn at home. He himself says that he was forced to look for a new position. . . . But Ercole II died on 3 October 1559, and his son

Alfonso II succeeded him. Cipriano now writes a letter to Alfonso, full of declarations and humble pleas, in which he offers his services to the young prince. This request, however, was not answered or was refused . . ."; *Ciprian de Rore*, p. 19. Solerti had merely remarked: "We do not know whether he was again welcomed in Ferrara" (*Ferrara e la Corte Estense*, pp. CXVII–CXVIII).

81. Alvin Johnson makes these valuable remarks: "On 10 October 1553 he was assigned rent-free residence and on 17 May 1556 a further expression of the Duke's high regard for Cipriano was materialized in a benefice to 'questo homo molto virtuoso et da bene et da molt' anni suo servitore'" ("The Liturgical Music," p. 25). The more astonishing that even after these signs of ducal benevolence Rore did not deviate from his principle not to dedicate a publication of his to the duke, let alone anyone else.

82. Bernhard Meier, in his study, "Staatskompositionen von Cyprian de Rore," *Tijdschrift van de Vereniging voor Nederlandse Muziekgeschiedenis*, XXI (1969), 81–118, ignores this passage and arrives at the conclusion that "Rore loved courtly atmosphere so much . . . that he exchanged the most honorable post that Venice could bestow on a composer, that of chapelmaster of San Marco, with the equivalent post at the court of Parma" (p. 81). Alfred Einstein had already explained sufficiently why Rore had left Venice: ". . . his health was apparently not robust enough to cope with his exacting duties at San Marco. Nor did he like the division of the choir [into *cappella grande* and *cappella piccola*] and the resulting disorder. Then, too, he found his salary insufficient" (*Italian Madrigal*, I, 388). See also Gustave Reese, *Music in the Renaissance*, rev. ed. (New York, 1959), p. 330. The question is obviously the reverse: if Rore loved courtly atmosphere so much, why did he leave the court of Parma for the Church of San Marco?

83. See Casimir von Chledowski, *Der Hof von Ferrara* (Berlin, 1918), p. 217. See also p. 470, where other court poets (Pistoia, Guarini), too, are cited as censuring the hypocrisy governing life at the court.

84. This portrait appears at the end of the luxurious manuscript of motets of Cipriano de Rore, Munich, Bayerische Staatsbibliothek, MS B, on the last folio. More than half the number of the

153 parchment leaves are illuminated with miniatures of Hans Mielich illustrating the text of the motets. See Jessie Ann Owens, "An Illuminated Manuscript of Motets by Cipriano de Rore (München, Bayerische Staatsbibliothek, Mus. MS. B)" (Ph.D. diss., Princeton University, 1979).

85. For Hol, see n. 79; for Einstein, *Italian Madrigal*, I, 384.

86. Johnson, "The 1548 Editions of Cipriano de Rore's Third Book of Madrigals," *Studies in Musicology in Honor of Otto E. Albrecht*, ed. John Walter Hill (Kassel, 1980), pp. 110–24; p. 112. The first book of 1544 is dedicated to "Signor Jheronimo Uttinger," not by Rore, but Antonio Gardane. The other two books of 1545 and 1549 carry no dedications. Alvin Johnson has shown that the same situation prevails in the publication of Rore's *Vergini* of 1548.

87. See Bernhard Meier's study cited in n. 82.

88. See Meier, "Staatskompositionen," pp. 88–90. For an edition of the chanson, see Meier, *Rore Opera omnia*, VIII, 39–43.

89. Meier, "Staatskompositionen," p. 88.

90. Einstein, *Italian Madrigal*, I, 392.

91. See n. 86.

92. That a child of thirteen should have been the model for Carpi's mature Venus seems to us surprising. Let us remember, though, that Anne of Brittany and Diane de Poitiers were fifteen years old when they married—and this was not uncommon at that time.

93. Ferrarese accounts record a payment to Carpi on the 26th of January 1544 "per il quadro . . . nominato la galatea" (Mezzetti, *Girolamo da Ferrara*, p. 58b). As I have hypothesized above, it is quite possible that Carpi's painting was known under this name at court. The 1743 inventory also calls it "un quadro con una Galatea" (see above, p. 12). The likelihood of the validity of both names is confirmed in reverse by Raphael's *Galatea*, painted for the Sienese banker Agostino Chigi in 1511–12; it was celebrated by Chigi's house poets as "the nascent Venus borne on the waves in a shell"; see *The Complete Work of Raphael* (New York, 1969), p. 160. Luisa Becherucci, in her contribution on "Raphael and Painting" (pp. 9–197), accompanies this

quotation with the remark that this "commonly is considered as an inexact allusion to Raphael's *Galatea*" (p. 160; see fig. 144, p. 125). Inexact or not, "Venus" and "Galatea" were apparently exchanged with ease at that time.

94. J. J. Pollitt, *The Art of Greece 1400–31 B.C., Sources and Documents* (Englewood Cliffs, N.J., 1965), pp. 165–66.

95. See E. H. Gombrich, "The Heritage of Apelles," title essay in *The Heritage of Apelles, Studies in the Art of the Renaissance* (Ithaca, 1976), p. 14.

96. Panofsky, *Studies in Iconology*, p. 153.

97. See James Hutton, *The Greek Anthology in Italy to the Year 1800* (Ithaca, 1935). Greek epigrams from the Anthology were copied by Angelo Poliziano (1454–94) perhaps as early as 1472 (see p. 124); he also wrote imitations in Greek and in Latin, two of which were devoted to *Venus Anadyomene* and *Venus Armata* (p. 140). To acquire an overview of the immense number of translations and imitations of Greek epigrams in Latin and Italian, it is sufficient to glance at Hutton's "Register" (pp. 443–649) of the *incipits* of verses; to obtain an idea of the eminence of Venus in these verses, see nos. 16.159–178 (pp. 634–38). From the incipits alone we can count a minimum of ten Latin epigrams on Praxiteles's Aphrodite of Knidos. Aphrodite had sanctuaries in Paphos and Cythera, hence her byname "Paphian Cythera."

98. Pollitt, *Art of Greece*, p. 131 (Pollitt's translation).

99. ". . . il Falletti scrisse dottamente in latino, e tradusse dal greco in italiano . . ." (Serafini, *Carpi*, p. 110).

100. See Ovid, *Metamorphoses*, with an English translation by Frank Justus Miller, 2 vols. (Cambridge and London, 1951), II, 296–97.

101. *Ibid.*, p. 456.

102. Serafini, *Carpi*, p. 110. For a critical assessment of Serafini's monograph, see F. Antal, "Observations on Girolamo da Carpi" (see n. 27 above).

103. See Aloïs Gerlo, *Erasme et ses portraitistes* (Nieuwkoop, 1969), after p. 8.

104. Mezzetti, *Girolamo da Ferrara*, p. 98.

105. See Lewis and Short, *A Latin Dictionary* (Oxford, 1966), p. 733.

106. The "vespe" are barely visible in the tree trunk on which Mars's head rests; that they are there one can see in ill. 50 of Gombrich's fascinating study on "Botticelli's Mythologies," where we are given an enlargement of the wasps and, in ill. 49, for comparison, the wasps of the Vespucci coat-of-arms. For the pertinent text, see p. 68.

107. See Lightbown, *Botticelli*, II, B41, pp. 55–56; see I, plate III for a color illustration of *Mars and Venus.*

108. Lowinsky, "Musical Genius—Evolution and Origins of a Concept," *The Musical Quarterly*, L (1964), 321–40 and 476–95; see p. 477.

109. *Ibid.*, p. 484.

110. The expression occurs in the *Dichiaratione* added by Monteverdi's brother Giulio Cesare to the fifth book of madrigals written at the behest of Claudio and expressing his ideas. For the original see G. Francesco Malipiero, *Claudio Monteverdi* (Milan, 1929), pp. 72–85; see p. 77; for an English translation see Oliver Strunk, *Source Readings in Music History* (New York, 1950), pp. 405–12; see p. 408. The passage reads in the original (Malipiero, p. 78): "Seconda prattica, de la quale è stato il primo rinovatore ne nostri caratteri il Divino Cipriano Rore . . . intende che sia quella che versa intorno alla perfetione della melodia, cioè che considera l'armonia comandata, e non comandante, e per signora dell'armonia pone l'oratione. . . ." One can find the translation in Strunk, who omitted, probably inadvertently, the word "Divino" in his version (pp. 408–9). To the term "perfettione della melodia," see G. B. Doni, who calls *melodia perfetta* that melody that is set to a text; see *Trattato primo sopra el genere enharmonico*, in G. B. Doni, *Lyra Barberina*, ed. Antonio Francesco Gori, I (Florence, 1763), 295.

111. *Discourse on Ancient Music*, ca. 1580 (Strunk, *Source Readings*, pp. 290–301; p. 295).

112. Romano Alberti, *Trattato della nobiltà della pittura* (Mantua, 1591), ed. Paola Barocchi in *Trattati d'Arte del Cinquecento*, 3 vols. (Bari, 1960–62), III, 211.

Endnotes to Excursus

1. Falletti had to rephrase the poem for the 1557 edition of his works, for there he began with a lengthy verse epic in four books, *De bello Sicambrico*. Having now "recited the battles" and "sung of the magnificent deeds," it was necessary to change the opening lines of the poem:

> Gelrhorum scripsi pugnas, atque inclyta magni
> Caesaris, aeternum quae vivent gesta per aevum.

> Written have I of the Gelrhi's battles and of the
> Deeds of the mighty Caesar, which shall live on forever.

Falletti's poem on music was later translated into Italian in the following publication: *Le Lodi della Musica Tradotte da i Versi Latini del Conte Girolamo Faletti In ottava rima, da Giovan Mario Verdezzotti. All'Illustrissimo & Eccellentissimo Signore D. Alfonso II Duca di Ferrara* (Venice, 1563). Here the poem begins:

> L'horrende pugne del Sicambro altero
> E di Cesar contai gli incliti gesti.
> Che malgrado del tempo invido, e fero
> Fien sempre al mondo chiari, e manifesti.

> I sang of the horrendous battles of the proud Sicambro
> And of Caesar's magnificent deeds
> Which in spite of Time's envy and fierceness,
> Shall forever remain manifest to the world and glorious.

The *bellum Sicambricum* is the war that the French started against Charles V in the Netherlands in 1542, at the time when Falletti studied at the University of Louvain, which made it possible for him to take part in the beginning of the armed conflict; see Girolamo Tiraboschi, *Storia della*

Letteratura Italiana, Vol. VII, Part 3 (Florence, 1812), p. 950. The *Gelrhi* are the people of Gelderland, a province of Eastern Netherlands. The mighty Caesar is of course Charles V.

Professor Arthur W. H. Adkins suggests that Falletti, in writing the lines "Describant alii pugnas . . . ," was stimulated by Virgil's famous verses toward the end of the *Aeneid* (VI, 847–853):

> Excudent alii spirantia mollius aera,
> (Credo equidem), vivos ducent de marmore voltus,
> Orabunt causas melius caelique meatus
> Describent radio et surgentia sidera dicent;
> Tu regere imperio populos, Romane, memento
> (Hae tibi erunt artes) pacisque imponere morem,
> Parcere subjectis et debellare superbos.

In Adkins' literal translation:

> Others will hammer out more softly
> The bronze so that it seems to breathe,
> Will draw forth living faces from the marble,
> Will plead cases better, and will display [indicate]
> The movements of the heavens with the geometer's staff,
> And will tell of the rising constellations.
> May [Do] you, O Roman, remember to govern the peoples
> With your rule (These shall be your arts)
> And enforce the habit of peace,
> To spare the conquered and subdue the proud.

For a free translation, see Charles E. Bennett, *Virgil's Aeneid Books I–VI*, Bennett's Latin Series

(Boston and Chicago, 1904), p. XIV.

2. A later source is *Hier. Faleti Poemata*, in *Delitiae CC. Italorum Poetarum . . . collectore Ranutio Ghero* (Frankfurt, 1608), I, 947ff.

3. Falletti assumes that Carpi's painting was done on wood. In fact, the work was made on canvas; see Mezzetti, *Girolamo da Ferrara*, p. 73b.

4. Add the mental note: "who take me for Venus."

5. Who is the "Phrygian judge"? A good guess would seem to be the first historical King Midas of Phrygia. Herodotus (I, 14) reports that he donated his throne of Justice, a rich and admirable work of art, to Delphi. This tells us two things: Midas was famous for wise judgments and he had good relations with the Greeks. See Pauly und Wissowa, *Real-Encyclopädie der classischen Altertumswissenschaft*, XXX (Stuttgart, 1932), cols. 1538–39.

Professor Adkins proposes a more convincing solution. In Virgil's *Aeneid*, Paris, who, appointed judge between Juno, Pallas, and Venus, selected the last as the most beautiful, is also called "Phrygius" (IV, 140). He would most naturally be the "Phrygian judge." This is confirmed in the poem of 1546 that is omitted in the edition of 1557:

Forma Deae est, facies melior Cythereide, Pallas
    Tristis adhuc, Phrygio nec satis equa viro.
Cur sibi tam similes pictor sub imagine vultus
    Effinxit? rursus provocet ut Venerem.

Her body is that of a goddess; her face excels Venus; even
    Pallas is disconsolate, for the Phrygian judges her not in her class.
Why did the painter portray her in the picture so similar to her?
    To produce another Venus.

The lines "even Pallas is disconsolate, for the Phrygian judges her not in her class" make sense only when "the Phrygian" is known to be Paris.

6. This is the same Pyrrhus Didacus who appears in Falletti's collection of 1557 as poetic correspondent with the author. He acts also as a participant in Lilio Gregorio Giraldi's *Dialogi duo de poetis nostrorum temporum* (Florence, 1551), reprinted in *Lilii Gregorii Gyraldi Ferrariensis Operum . . . Tomi duo* (Basel, 1580), II, 378–421. Each participant in the dialogues has to report about a certain national literature. Didacus, introduced by Giraldi as "a man at home in history and mythology, and fluent in Greek and Latin" (*memorem hominem historiarum, ac fabularum et bene graece et latine scientem*; p. 379), was asked to speak about Spanish and English poets of the period because he was widely travelled. Didacus Pyrrhus, alias Diego Pires of Portugal, was "one of the many Jews attracted to Ferrara by the prevailing climate of religious toleration"; P. R. Horne, *The Tragedies of Giambattista Cinthio Giraldi* (Oxford, 1962), p. 12.

The Jews in Ferrara enjoyed more privileges than in other states. On February 12, 1550, Ercole II issued a general safe conduct to Spanish and Portuguese Jews, and in a letter of patent assured the immigrants that they shall be treated as citizens ("Siano trattati come cittadini"). That their lot was nevertheless precarious in the presence of the Church, the Inquisition, and the economic crises, in which they were invariably made scapegoats, can be followed in the well-documented book of Andrea Balletti, *Gli Ebrei e gli Estensi* (Reggio Emilia, 1930). The above quotation occurs on pp. 77–78.

7. Among the poems Falletti and Pyrrhus exchanged there is one in Falletti's collection of 1557 (fol. 104) entitled: *Ad Didacum Pyrrhum Lusitanum,* in which these two lines occur:

Verum cara tamen ita sunt tua carmina Pyrrhe,
    Illis ut possit gratius esse nihil.

Truly, so dear indeed are your poems to me, Pyrrhus,
    That there is nothing that could please me more.

8. Lilio Gregorio Giraldi mentions him in his two dialogues *De poetis nostrorum temporum* (*Operum*, II, 414).

9. Gibbons, *Dosso and Battista Dossi*, p. 223. See above, p. 12. Gibbons could have known at least six of Falletti's eleven poems from Serafini's book on Carpi (pp. 90 and 127).

10. On his *Historiae poetarum tam graecorum quam latinorum dialogi decem* of 1545, see Bernard Weinberg, A *History of Literary Criticism in the Italian Renaissance*, 2 vols. (Chicago, 1961), I, 104–6.

11. Page 378; on p. 377 appears a dedication to the Duchess of Ferrara, Renata (Renée) of France. She too receives a eulogy in verse.

12. ". . . coepimus de Nuptijs Annae Esten(sis) nostrorum principum filiae, Virginis lectissimae, & omni virtute, & elegantia Principe digna praeditae, quae tunc celebrabantur, inter nos agere. Cuius Ill(ustrissimae) puellae raras animi & corporis dotes, non brevius commemorare possim quam his hendecasyllabis, quos in eius imaginem à Carpensi nostro pictore superioribus mensibus depictam composueram."

13. ". . . il dono . . . dei ritratti di tutti i figli del Duca dipinti da Girolamo da Carpi"; see Mezzetti, *Girolamo da Ferrara*, p. 61a.

14. *De bello Sicambrico*, fol. cv^{v}.